Introducti...

The Vikings called it *Dyfflin*, from the ... meaning Black Pool. Black Pool was a deep and dark body of water behind Dublin Castle. Dubh Linn became, in time, Dublin.

James Joyce, fascinated by the River Liffey and the city through which it flowed, adorned both with many names in his novel, *Finnegans Wake*. The Liffey, or *Anna Livia* as it is affectionately named in Joyce's novel, rises in the Wicklow Mountains and ambles slowly through County Kildare on its journey towards Dublin Bay. Near where it enters the sea a city was born, over 1,000 years ago. Once, the city was a strongly fortified medieval town with an international trading reputation. Much later, the city became one of the most squalid and poverty-stricken cities in Europe. In between, it was, for a time, one of the great European capitals, the second most important city in the vast British Empire.

Today, Dublin is an exciting, modern city with an intriguing past. It is the capital of a young, independent, democratic Republic. It has, once again, moved onto the European stage. It is a city which is changing and developing, re-inventing itself over and over again. Visitors discover quickly the two sides to this magnificent European capital: the beauty and fascination of its sometimes troubled past, and the unmistakable feeling of a living city once again economically focused and forging ahead in arts and culture.

About This Book

It is with much pleasure that we present to you the **Dublin Pocket Guide**.

Almost everything you need to know about the city is contained in these pages. From the opening section, **Dublin Origins**, to the concluding **Directory**, you will discover much about Dublin's past and plenty of information on Dublin's present. **Things You Should Know About Dublin** and **Essential Visitor Information** are both practical sections addressing a wide variety of subjects (customs, money, banks, post, the economy, the political system, language, religion, etc). **Arts and Culture** is devoted to Dublin's famous writers, musicians, actors, directors, artists and architects, while access transport and transport around the city are dealt with in **Getting To And Around Dublin**, as well as information on organised tours of the city and its environs. **Things To See And Do** is the largest section of the Guide and contains 74 individual entries, each with detailed information to help you appreciate your visit. Opening times and admission charges are included with each entry.

We have included three detailed **Walking Tours**: *18th-Century Dublin*, *Medieval Dublin*, *Dublin Pubs*. Each Tour is accompanied by an easy-to-follow map. The five separate **Day and Half-Day Excursions Outside Dublin** are recognised as classic excursions. At the back of the Guide the detailed **Directory** contains information on **Accommodation**, **Dining Out**, **Shopping**, **Entertainment**, **Sports**, and **Annual Events in Dublin**.

Combine the above information with a reader-friendly layout and design - which includes maps of the city centre and of the Greater Dublin Area - and illustrate the entire book with photographs from award-winning Peter Zoeller, and you have in your possession *the perfect pocket companion*.

Contents

This Is Dublin - First Published 1994. 2nd Edition 1996. 3rd Edition 1997. 4th Edition 1999
Produced by: Language & Publishing Partnership, 65 Abberley, Shanganagh Road, Killiney, Co. Dublin. Tel: (01) 2827866. Fax: (01) 2720227. E Mail: langpp@iol.ie.
Production Director: Steve White. **Author:** Gerry Boland.
Design & Layout: Pure Drop Productions (White).
Colour Reproduction: The Type Bureau.
Printed by: Edelvives, Spain.
Copyright © Steve White & Gerry Boland 1999.
Published by Gill & Macmillan Ltd, Goldenbridge, Dublin 8 with associated companies throughout the world.

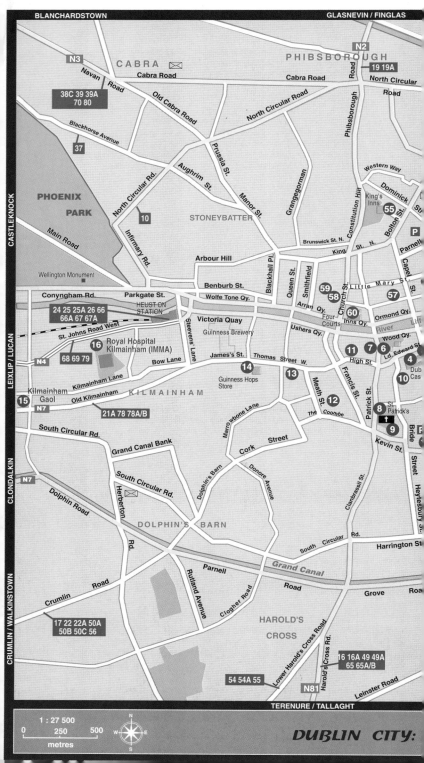

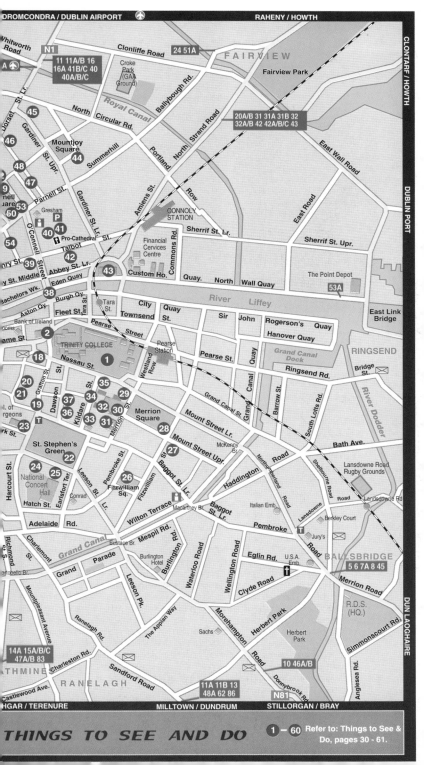

Whitworth Road

N1

11 11A/B 16
16A 41B/C 40
40A/B/C

Clonliffe Road

24 51A

FAIRVIEW

Croke Park
(GAA Ground)

Fairview Park

Dorset St.

45

46

48

47

53

50

54

Gardiner St. Upr.

Mountjoy Square

44

Summerhill

North Circular Rd.

Royal Canal

Ballybough Rd.

Portland Row

North Strand Road

20A/B 31 31A 31B 32
32A/B 42 42A/B/C 43

East Wall Road

East Road

Parnell St.

Gardiner St. Lr.

Amiens St.

CONNOLLY STATION

Sherrif St. Lr.

Sherrif St. Upr.

Gresham

P
i
40

41

Pro-Cathedral

Talbot St.

42

Financial Services Centre

Commons Rd.

O'Connell Street

39

Abbey St. Lr.

Eden Quay

43

Custom Ho.

Quay. North Wall Quay

The Point Depot

53A

St. Middle

Bachelors Wk.

Burgh Qy.

38

Aston Qy.

Fleet St.

Tara St.

Bank of Ireland

me St.

2

18

Fleet St.

Tara St.

City Quay

Townsend St.

River Liffey

Sir John Rogerson's Quay

Hanover Quay

East Link Bridge

TRINITY COLLEGE

1

Nassau St.

Pearse Street

Pearse Station

Westland Row

Pearse St.

Grand Canal Quay

Ringsend Rd.

RINGSEND

Bridge St.

River Dodder

20

21

19

23

Grafton St.

37

34

36

Dawson St.

Kildare St.

35

33

32

30

31

29

Merrion St.

Merrion Square

28

Mount Street Lr.

Grand Canal St.

Barrow St.

South Lotts Rd.

Grand Canal Dock

l. of rgeons

T

rk St.

St. Stephen's Green

22

24

25

National Concert Hall

Hatch St.

Harcourt St.

Leeson St. Lr.

Earlsfort Ter.

Pembroke St.

26

Fitzwilliam Sq.

Conrad

27

Mount Street Upr.

Baggot St. Lr.

McKenny Br.

Haddington Road

Northumberland Road

Shelbourne Road

Bath Ave.

Lansdowne Road Rugby Grounds

Lansdowne Rd

Adelaide Rd.

Wilton Terrace

i

Macartney Br.

Baggot St. Lr.

Italian Emb.

Pembroke Road

Lansdowne Road

Berkley Court

Jury's

T

BALLSBRIDGE

5 6 7A 8 45

Richmond S.

rtobello Br

Charlemont St.

Grand Parade

Mespil Rd.

Burlington Hotel

Eustace Br.

Grand

Leeson Pk.

Burlington Rd.

Waterloo Road

Wellington Road

Eglin Rd.

Clyde Road

U.S.A. Emb.

i

Merrion Road

R.D.S. (HQ.)

Simmonscourt Rd.

Grand Canal

THMINE

14A 15A/B/C
47A/B 83

RANELAGH

Ranelagh Rd.

Charleston Rd.

Mountpleasant Avenue

The Appian Way

Sachs

Morehampton Road

Herbert Park

Herbert Park

Anglesea Rd.

Castlewood Ave.

Sandford Road

HGAR / TERENURE

MILLTOWN / DUNDRUM

11A 11B 13
48A 62 86

Donnybrook Rd.

N81

STILLORGAN / BRAY

10 46A/B

DUN LAOGHAIRE

THINGS TO SEE AND DO

1 – 60 Refer to: Things to See & Do, pages 30 - 61.

Dublin Origins

River Liffey looking west with Ha'penny Bridge in foreground.   Photo: Peter Zoeller.

Before A City Was Born - Early Settlers

About six thousand years before the Vikings sailed into Dublin Bay for the first recorded time in AD 837, mesolithic hunter-gatherers were scouring the unblemished landscape for whatever food they could catch or find. Later, neolithic (New Stone Age) farmers introduced an organised system of farming, especially in the Boyne Valley region, north of Dublin. These people had brought across the sea from Wales and Scotland livestock and seeds for sowing crops. They left behind some awesome megalithic monuments, none more so than the cluster of passage-graves of Newgrange, Dowth and Knowth in the Boyne Valley, all constructed about five thousand years ago. The Bronze Age, which began some time before 2000 BC, saw the development of the use of copper and bronze material, for weaponry and ornamentation. Ireland was a major producer of copper and gold during this period and some of this exquisite work can be seen today in the National Museum in Dublin. When the Celts arrived in Ireland around 700 BC they brought with them a sophisticated lifestyle and culture and their influence spread throughout the country.

Many centuries later - the year was AD 432 - **St Patrick** arrived in Ireland. His arrival signified the coming of Christianity to Ireland. The ensuing four hundred years, a period often referred to as The Golden Age of Irish History, saw the remarkable development of a monastic culture throughout Ireland. Dublin Bay provided the setting for many monasteries and hermetic cells, from Howth Head straddling the north of the Bay to Dalkey Island on the south, and throughout the inland region, especially along the banks of the Rivers Liffey, Poddle, and Tolka. Along the River Poddle a church dedicated to St Patrick was built. This was later to achieve cathedral status under the Normans although the historic River Poddle has long since diminished in size and in fact now flows underneath Dublin city, unseen and largely forgotten by its modern-day inhabitants.

During the monastic period, the land where modern Dublin lies was a large flood plain where the River Liffey, then unhindered by man's engineering enterprises, meandered and spread at will. Much of O'Connell Street and the lands now occupied by Trinity College were submerged at high tide. Where now the gracious 18th-century Merrion Square so rightly commands respect in the fashionable Georgian district south-east of Trinity, there once lapped the waters of the incoming tide. At low tide one could see the marsh extend east from there to Ringsend. Today, the only water you will find on a walk from Merrion Square to Ringsend is that imported to fill the man-made Grand Canal. The Liffey, its flow squeezed and hindered by quayside intrusions along its banks, was then a wide and shallow expanse of flowing water, almost 300 metres in width at some points. At low tide, the naked beach was dotted with huge mud banks.

Áth Cliath

Near where the Vikings founded the small settlement which was to grow into Ireland's capital city, a makeshift, though thoroughly functional bridge traversed the River Liffey. This crossing was called Áth Cliath (the town of the ford of the hurdles). It consisted of mounds of stones at regular intervals over which was placed logs and branches to form the only bridge across the Liffey. Today, the Gaelic name for Dublin is Baile Átha Cliath (the town of the hurdleford). Áth Cliath was built near a very important junction, where three great long-distance highways crossed: the Slige Mór to the west, the Slige Midluachra to the north, and the Slige Chualann to the south. At low tide travellers along the north-south route availed of the man-made crossing. Above Áth Cliath to the south, on the small yet strategic hill which overlooks the river, was located the 6th-century church of St Columcille, replaced in the 12th century by that of St Audoen, remains of which can still be seen today.

The Vikings

The small population scattered around the hill overlooking Áth Cliath were no match for the fierce Norse Viking warriors whose lifestyle was based on raiding and plundering. Being sea-faring people, they were constantly on the waves, calling at different ports throughout Europe, trading goods and slaves. Before they arrived into Dublin Bay and established a *longphort* in AD 841, Viking longboats had made raids for more than a decade along the east coast of Ireland. In 837, sixty-five ships sailed into Dublin Bay, but their arrival four years later was to prove decisive, because, even though the 841 raiders left Dublin in 902 for reasons not entirely clear, when they returned fifteen years later they set up a trading town which was, this time, to be permanent. They established themselves in a different location, on top of the hill which overlooked Áth Cliath and which today can be identified as the area stretching from Christ Church Cathedral to Dublin Castle.

Over time, many of these nomadic semi-settlers put down permanent roots in the bustling, energetic, trading towns they had established. Dublin was no different. Within the walls of this emerging urban unit a settled, Viking population began to grow. Outside the walls, notably to the west, suburbs developed where today runs Thomas Street and St James's Gate (Guinness Brewery). By 1100, the walled area of the town was about 12 hectares. Most houses were made of wood and an average house measured 8.5 by 4.75 m. The most impressively built structures were the churches, of which there were many - a result of the diverse population which the new town attracted. Archaeological surveys and excavations have confirmed the existence of an enormous Viking cemetery west of Áth Cliath, stretching north and north-west from one of Dublin's main train termini, Heuston Station. Reckoned to be the largest Viking cemetery outside of Scandinavia, it was discovered some 150 years ago and confirms that Dublin had become in the 11th and 12th centuries a town housing a significant Viking population.

Not all was sweetness and light, however. There were many efforts to oust the Vikings, not least the *Battle of Dublin* in 919, fought out upstream from Heuston Station on the Liffey at Islandbridge. During this battle, the King of Tara was slain and his warriors routed by the superior military forces of the Vikings. Less than 100 years later, in the legendary 1014 *Battle of Clontarf*, the Vikings, who were allied to the province of Leinster and whose forces were augmented by overseas assistance, were decisively defeated by the Irish High King, Brian Boru. Although their power was curtailed, the Vikings continued to be a forceful presence in Dublin life. That is, until the Anglo-Normans arrived in Dublin.

The Normans

In 1166 Dublin acknowledged the high kingship of Rory O'Connor, high king of Connacht. The deposed Dermot MacMurrough was driven overseas and, in his efforts to re-establish himself as high king, he asked King Henry II for assistance. Richard de Clare (**Strongbow**) was summoned and on 23 August 1169 he arrived off the Wexford coast with 200 knights and 1,000 soldiers. He took control of Dublin, marrying in the process MacMurrough's daughter, Eva, thus consolidating his position. However, when MacMurrough died in 1171, Henry II, fearing Strongbow's ambitions to gain authority over the whole island, curbed them when he arrived in Ireland with an army which, by its sheer size, dissuaded any Irish

Dublin City Coat of Arms.
Photo: Peter Zoeller.

chieftain from offering armed resistance. He spent four months in Dublin, built a temporary palace to express his power and influence, and left Ireland having asserted his authority over the entire country. He dissolved Strongbow's ambitions by granting him the province of Leinster, and outmanouevered him by cleverly granting Dublin's first charter to the city of Bristol, appointing Hugh de Lacy as its first governor. From now on Dublin was to play a central role in the English government's endeavours in Ireland, only ending with Irish independence in 1922.

From this time on the physical structure and size of the city began to change in many ways. The city walls were fortified and additional gateways and towers were built, all aimed at making the city secure against outside attack. The foundations of Christ Church Cathedral were begun in 1172, and the imposing Dublin Castle was begun in 1205. Outside the walls, St Patrick's Church received cathedral status in 1220, and the Liberties, a collection of independent suburbs in the vicinity of St Patrick's, began to exert influence over the city authorities. Near Dublin Castle, where the Rivers Poddle and Liffey converged, a body of listless, dark water lay. The Vikings had called this pool *Dyfflin*, or *Dubh Linn*, meaning *Black Pool*, a name later to be anglicised as Dublin. This strongly fortified city comprised an area of forty-four acres. Its occupants were constantly on their guard against fire, a frequent and devastating visitor, and disease, the worst example of which was the Black Death which swept through the city in 1348, wiping out many thousands of inhabitants.

Important 16th- and 17th-Century Events

In 1534, 'Silken' Thomas Fitzgerald staged an insurrection which was assertively put down by the then King of England, Henry VIII. Three years later, Henry's *Act of Supremacy* made him the self-styled King of Ireland and head of the Church. The continued suppression of Gaelic culture, religion and language was an obvious result and this suppression was given added encouragement during the dominant reign of **Queen Elizabeth I** (1558-1603). Her objective was, quite simply, to establish an Irish colony, and her efforts to succeed in this brought her down the road of human plantations, a policy which was to transform the socio-political landscape for ever more. In Dublin, Elizabeth left her mark in the form of Trinity College, the university which she founded in 1592, its educational purpose being the 'planting of learning, the increasing of civility, and the establishing of true religion within the realm', i.e. Protestantism.

After his unceremonious rout of the King of England, Oliver Cromwell directed his awesome appetite for conquest at Ireland. He landed in Dublin in August 1649 and quickly set about conquering the entire island, slaughtering many thousands of men, women and children in the process. In a famous, chilling phrase, he ordered all 'transplantable' Irish persons *to Hell or to Connaught* (Ireland's westerly and most barren province). Towards the end of the century, the Catholic ex-King of England, James II fought and lost a significant battle when he was defeated by the Protestant King William of Orange (King Billy) at the Battle of the Boyne in 1690.

18th-Century Dublin

Population estimates put Dublin's at 10,000 inhabitants in 1600, a smaller city than London, York, Bristol, Norwich or Edinburgh. One hundred years later it had risen to 60,000, and by the turn of the following century, in 1800, Dublin had become the second largest city in the British Isles and among the largest cities in Europe, outside of London, Paris, Vienna, Naples and perhaps Amsterdam. Its population was 180,000 and it contained an array of magnificent public buildings that were the envy of every city in Europe. In addition, it had become an important centre of theatre and music, and a wide range of publishing and service industries flourished.

This remarkable development was due to the increased confidence of the Protestant ascendancy. Their position in Dublin society had been

Georgian Houses on Merrion Square.   Photo: Peter Zoeller.

rising in direct proportion to the descending fortunes of the ancient Catholic aristocracy, both Gaelic and Old English. This Catholic aristocracy had suffered as a result of the Reformation and the wars of the 17th century and were, by the early 18th century, a disenfranchised and disillusioned class. The vacuum they left was filled with great aplomb and tremendous industrial zeal by the Protestant ascendancy.

The city grew in status. The large, elegant and exquisitely decorated houses which were built north and south of the River Liffey were essentially for an aristocratic society: people of high social status and prominent political figures. On the south side, the most important houses were around St Stephen's Green, and along the streets leading off - Leeson Street, Harcourt Street, Ely Place and Hume Street.

Jonathan Swift
(1667-1745)

Important houses were built also on nearby South William Street, Dawson Street, Molesworth Street and Kildare Street. On the north of the city, Rutland (now Parnell) Square and Sackville Mall (now O'Connell Street) were laid out, and Gardiner's Row and North Great George's Street extended the district further. Some of Dublin's most elegant and individual Georgian houses can be seen on these fine streets today. The Commissioners for Wide Streets (established in 1757) brought about the transformation of the city even further. Sackville Mall was extended to the Liffey and a bridge was built to meet the newly created Westmoreland Street. By this sweeping and imaginative development the city's axis moved eastwards as people could now cross the river at a more easterly point.

During this development **Jonathan Swift** (1667-1745), author of *Gulliver's Travels*, was Dean of St Patrick's Cathedral from 1713 to 1745. In 1742, the composer Handel conducted the public premiere of his *Messiah* in the old, now demolished, music hall on

Fishamble Street, beside Christ Church Cathedral. The Irish Parliament, in its new and majestic home on College Green, was encouraged by Henry Grattan's Patriot Party to demand the repeal of the anti-Catholic Penal Code in 1778, and four years later Grattan's Parliament, as it became known, persuaded the British Parliament to declare the executive and judicial independence of Ireland. During Grattan's Parliament the city continued to prosper, but Dublin's fortunes were soon to change.

The Act of Union in 1800 and the subsequent demise of Dublin

Two years after the unsuccessful 1798 rebellion against the English Crown, a rebellion which was inspired by the charismatic political figure, **Wolfe Tone** (1763-98), the Act of Union was passed, abolishing Ireland's Parliament and implanting direct rule from London. The Union Jack was raised above Bedford Tower in Dublin Castle. The immediate result was that much of Dublin's aristocracy moved out, beating a hasty retreat from the city which had lost its political independence and was as a result losing economic momentum and social significance rapidly. The bustling city which, during the latter half of the 18th century had become a place of international trading importance, quickly lost direction.

At this time there was a crisis in the physical state of housing within the Liberties area of the city. By 1860, the houses, especially those in the teeming alleys and courts, were quite literally falling down. As the fine houses of Mountjoy Square, Gardiner's Row and other 18th-century developments emptied of their aristocratic landlords, poor families, who had been living in houses which were on the point of falling down, moved - lock, stock and barrel - into the empty shells of these Georgian gems of architecture. Dublin's growth in population did not slow down at this time - rather, between 1798 and 1821, some 40,000 inhabitants were added to its population. These people simply moved in to the empty houses out of necessity. By occupying them during a period of economic decline, and, by their presence, causing a severe devaluation of property in this once fashionable part of north Dublin city, they unwittingly kept the 19th-century developers' attention focussed on the emerging suburbs of Sandymount, Ballsbridge, Donnybrook, Ranelagh, Rathmines and Rathgar. Otherwise these magnificent Georgian houses of north Georgian Dublin might have fallen to clear the way for more modern development.

Dublin in the latter half of the 19th century and in the early 1900s was widely acknowledged as the most unhealthy city in the British Isles. This did not happen overnight. It had always had a very large population living in abject poverty. One-third of its population lived in one-roomed tenement accommodation, compared to less than ten per cent in London. Their taking up residence in the great houses and transforming them into tenements simply made them more visible.The 18th-century architectural fabric of the city remained intact because developers saw no sense in clearing the Georgian tenements in order to attract a well-to-do landlord. Well-to-do landlords were not interested in speculating in a city laden with tenements. Thus, by the end of the 19th century, Dublin was noted throughout Europe for its poverty and its tenements, whereas, 100 years earlier it had been noted for its wealth and elegance.

Ireland after the Act of Union was in political turmoil and there was widespread unrest among its citizenry. The minority Protestant ruling class and the powerless Catholic majority were both disillusioned, for different reasons of course. **Robert Emmet** (1778-1803), a young idealist much influenced by Wolfe Tone, attempted to capture Dublin Castle in 1803. His poorly organised rebellion was put down easily and he was sentenced to hang outside St Catherine's Church on Thomas Street. At his trial he made a moving speech which was to guarantee him a place among the romantic heroes of Ireland's long struggle for independence. 'Let no man write my epitaph ... When my country takes her place among the nations of the earth, then, and not till then, let my epitaph be written.'

The Famine

Irish farmers depended on the potato for their livelihood. Thus, when blight hit the crop from 1845 to 1848, the entire country was plunged into famine. In the space of a decade, the country lost two million people, approximately one-half dying from starvation and the other half emigrating to avoid almost certain starvation at home. Many of these forced emigrants, desperately ill and malnourished when boarding, died on the *coffin ships* which were taking them to America, Canada, Australia, New Zealand and England. Thousands of people from rural Ireland, in an attempt to escape from the tragedy which was unfolding in the countryside, descended on the capital. Here, death was commonplace as the workhouses became overcrowded and diseases such as cholera and typhus spread throughout the city.

Two Great 19th-Century Leaders

Two of the most important Irish political figures made their mark on Irish history in the 19th century. **Daniel O'Connell** (1775-1847), known as 'The Liberator', pursued his quest for Catholic Emancipation, founding the Catholic Association in 1823 and becoming the first Catholic to be elected to the British House of Parliament in 1828. A year later, limited voting rights were granted to Catholics. Later in the century, **Charles Stewart Parnell** (1846-91), a Protestant who was elected to Westminster in 1875, became leader of the Home Rule Party and advanced the rights of the depressed and discriminated Catholic tenants throughout Ireland. His outstanding leadership

Daniel O'Connell Statue.   Photo: Peter Zoeller.

12

and great popularity finally fell apart after he lost a broad section of public support following revelations of his relationship with Kitty O'Shea, the wife of a Captain O'Shea. He subsequently lost the leadership of his party and died soon after, at the age of forty-five.

Cultural Revival

Towards the end of the century a sense of an Irish identity was finding expression in popular bodies such as the Gaelic Athletic Association (GAA)(1884) and the Gaelic League (1893). Both organisations, in their own way, reflected a revival in interest in the Irish language and all aspects of Irish culture. The poet **William Butler Yeats** (1865-1939) was a central figure in the literary renaissance which saw the

James Joyce Statue.
Photo: Peter Zoeller.

foundation of the Abbey Theatre in 1904 and the emergence of writers such as John Millington Synge, George Moore, Lady Gregory, George Russell (AE), and some time later the genius of **James Joyce** (1882-1941). In Dublin, Arthur Griffith founded a newspaper called the *United Irishman.* This newspaper represented the views of **Sinn Féin**, meaning *Ourselves Alone* (founded in 1906) which sought an independent parliament in Dublin. In 1913, the Irish Volunteers were founded, to become the Irish Republican Army three years later.

1916 - The Easter Rising

On Bank Holiday Monday, 24 April 1916, some two thousand volunteers led by **Patrick Pearse** and **James Connolly** took control temporarily of fourteen strategic buildings in Dublin. The headquarters of the rebellion was the General Post Office (GPO) on O'Connell Street. Pearse read out a proclamation declaring Ireland an independent republic. Six days later, 20,000 British troops had captured all the rebels, their heavy artillery demolishing much of O'Connell Street in the process. The Dublin public was dismayed by the devastation in the city and displayed openly its hostility to the Volunteers and their 'fanatical' cause.

The British government made a grave error of judgment in the immediate aftermath of the Rising. In choosing to punish the leaders of the Rising in as stern a fashion as possible they played into the hands of those seeking Irish independence. Between 3 and 12 May, fifteen Volunteers were executed by firing squad, one of them, a crippled James Connolly, shot while tied to a chair. Sympathy for the Volunteers' cause spread throughout the country and the seeds were laid for a bloody struggle which would eventually lead to Independence, thus ending, at least in the twenty-six county State which emerged, an almost eight hundred year bitter-sweet relationship with the country which had had designs on Ireland since Henry II granted Dublin by Charter to the citizens of Bristol in 1172.

Independence and Civil War

In 1918, the re-emerging Sinn Féin Party swept the country in a landslide election which was particularly symbolic - over half of its candidates were in Irish and English jails at the time. The first Irish Parliament was declared in 1919, in Dublin's Mansion House, and this effectively left England with only one option - to put down this rising tide of nationalism. This they tried to do by sending over troops who had returned from the First World War. These troops became known as the *Black and Tans* on account of the colour of their uniform, and they waged an uncompromising war with the nationalist guerrillas throughout the country. In Dublin, the most infamous event of this period was *Bloody Sunday*, when soldiers fired indiscriminately into a capacity crowd attending a Gaelic football match in Croke Park, killing twelve people. This was in retaliation for the killing in Dublin that same morning of eleven British intelligence agents. In another part of the city, in May 1921, the IRA burned to a shell Dublin's finest public building and at the time the centre of British administration in Ireland, the Custom House.

Almost inevitably, a treaty was agreed upon and signed between the British government and representatives of the Irish 'Parliament'. The Anglo-Irish Treaty was signed on 6 December 1921 and was immediately described by Prime Minister Lloyd George as 'one of the greatest days in the history of the British Empire'. It was carried in the Dáil by sixty-four votes to fifty-seven in an uncompromising debate, and immediately afterwards the leader of Sinn Féin and President of Dáil Éireann, **Eamon de Valera** (1882-1975), rejected the Treaty out of hand - it excluded the six counties of Northern Ireland - and resigned from office. Many believed the Treaty was the most that could have been achieved in the circumstances and that it was only a matter of time before the six counties of Northern Ireland joined the south in a united Ireland. Others saw the treaty for what it was, a clever manoeuvre by Lloyd George to attempt to satisfy simultaneously the aspirations of the people south and north of Ireland.

The moment had passed. Men who, months earlier, had been fighting the Black and Tans side by side, were now divided on the Treaty. Families throughout Ireland were split on the issue. Inevitably, the country was plunged into civil war, in June 1922. The new, pro-Treaty government executed seventy-seven anti-treaty republicans in its first six months in office. In Dublin, part of the historic and splendid Four Courts was badly damaged in a fire which destroyed the Public Records Office and, with it, irreplaceable and important deeds and titles of great antiquity. In May 1923, de Valera gave up the armed struggle and in 1926 founded a new political party, Fianna Fáil (Soldiers of Destiny), which came to power in 1932. A new Constitution came into effect in 1938, effectively cementing Ireland's transition from a colony into an Independent Free State, Éire.

The Recent Past

De Valera steered Ireland through the Second World War as a neutral State. In 1949 Ireland formally became the Republic of Ireland. Throughout the 1950s Dublin muddled through a period of economic depression. Thousands of families were caught in a dire poverty trap: they were a constant reminder that achieving independence didn't automatically mean a better life for all citizens. Trinity College was still an educational establishment associated with Protestants, the Catholic Church persisting with its ban on Catholics attending the university.

The 1960s brought a steady improvement in the economy and in 1972 Ireland was accepted into the then European Economic Community (EEC). The economy grew, emigration decreased and Dublin's physical make-up began to change with the surge of road, housing and office development. Much of this change, in retrospect, was for the worse, as faceless and often ugly office blocks testify today. These office blocks often replaced dilapidated yet graceful 18th- and 19th-century houses and sometimes complete terraces. In the worst example, twenty-six original and intact Georgian houses on the perfectly-preserved Fitzwilliam Street were demolished and replaced by a new office complex, totally destroying the 18th-century uniformity of the street. The newly formed Georgian Society had mounted constant protests against this development, in the end to no avail. The city expanded and populous satellite suburbs were created, eating up green belt areas as more and more families moved out of the inner city. In the city centre a physical vacuum was created when, during Easter 1966, Dublin's O'Connell Street lost the towering column of Admiral Nelson in an IRA explosion. The loss of Nelson Pillar was a physical blow to the street. No building or monument since has managed to recapture the presence of *the Pillar*, as it was known, though plans to replace it with another kind of towering monument have been approved.

The Northern problem manifested itself in the Republic in its most hideous of forms when twenty-five civilians were murdered in three car-bomb explosions in Dublin on 17 May 1974. Two years earlier, angry crowds had stormed and petrol-bombed the British Embassy in Dublin following the infamous *Bloody Sunday* massacre in which thirteen people on a civil rights march in Derry City were shot dead by the British Army. Since the early 1970s, the Republic has been fortunate to escape the deadly shootings and bombings which have been a continuous feature of life in Northern Ireland since 1969. In all, over three thousand people have been killed in what is commonly called *The Troubles* in the North.

Dublin Today

Dublin today is a vibrant city. Its young population has found a cultural and social niche for itself in one of the most culturally aware cities in the world. The ever-present influence of past and present figures in the sphere of arts and culture, coupled with a political recognition of the need to assist the arts financially, has opened many young minds to the possibility of a career in these areas.

Politically, the Government is a stable one, perhaps not offering many long-term solutions to the economic and social challenges which face the nation, but a stable government is a luxury the country had been without throughout the 1980s and early 1990s. The financial benefits of participation in the European Union are substantial. Ireland has to date been a net beneficiary of European funds, though a combination of the growth of the Celtic Tiger economy in Ireland, coupled with the pressures for a diversion of European monies towards

The River Liffey.   Photo: Peter Zoeller.

the economies of Eastern Europe, are about to change this situation completely.

As with all Western economies, unemployment is a problem that will not go away and Dubliners suffer particularly greatly in this respect. Nationwide, unemployment is running at about 9% of the workforce, however in some unemployment *blackspots* in Dublin, over 50% of the local workforce is long-term unemployed. Many families live below the recognised poverty line. Like most modern cities, petty and violent crime is growing, and much of this is related to a growing drug addiction problem in some areas of the city. On the other side of the coin, the fashionable areas of the city are becoming more and more fashionable as influences from continental Europe steadily seep into the Dublin scene.

Emigration has been an integral part of Irish life since the Famine, though many of today's emigrants are leaving for different reasons than their predecessors: to earn more, to gain experience, to travel and to enjoy other cultures. Sadly, despite the Celtic Tiger and its overall effect on the Irish economy, a large number of emigrants still leave Ireland because they cannot find work at home. At Christmas time, cities, towns and villages throughout Ireland are thronged with the homecomers and in Dublin, on Christmas Eve, the pedestrianised and highly fashionable Grafton Street takes on the air of a small village as returning Dubliners literally bump into friends unseen since the previous Christmas.

Symbolising the mood of social change which swept through urban and rural Ireland in the 1990s, **Mary Robinson,** a liberal thinker and a social reformer, was elected the first woman President of Ireland in November 1990. Her election and the subsequent election of Northern Ireland-born **Mary McAleese** in November 1997 as her successor, signalled many changes ahead for a country wrapped up in a diverse baggage of traditional values. At the centre of this transformation is Dublin, ever-present, ever-changing, a European city of renewed stature, an Irish city coping with the needs of a constantly changing society.

Things You Should Know About Dublin

Topography and Climate

There are 32 counties in the island of Ireland and 26 of these comprise the Republic. The island is divided into four provinces: the nine counties of Ulster in the north; the six counties of Munster in the south; the five counties of Connacht in the west; and the twelve counties of Leinster in the east. Dublin City is the capital of the Republic of Ireland. It is also the capital of Co. Dublin, which county is one of the 12 counties of Leinster. County Dublin is located in the southern half of the only extensive coastal lowland in Ireland. In the north of the county gently rolling landscapes caress the fertile Central Lowlands and the historic Boyne Valley, while in the south the Dublin-Wicklow mountain massif keeps guard over the vale of Dublin below. The River Liffey, rising in the Wicklow Mountains, winds its way down to Dublin City and through its centre into Dublin Bay.

It is said that in Dublin it is common to experience the four seasons in one day, such are the perceived sudden variations in climate. This is an old wives' tale, but like all such tales, there is an element of truth in it. The climate, by and large, is relatively mild. A typical winter's day (November to February) is brisk (between 5°C and 10 °C), with a risk of rain. A summer's day, by contrast, is warmer (between 14 and 20°C), with a risk of rain. You are likely to enjoy more sunshine in May and June than at any other time of year, and more cloudy days in December.

Finding Your Feet

The main axis of the city is from north to south, from the wide O'Connell Street, across the River Liffey at O'Connell Bridge, through College Green with Trinity College on your left and the Bank of Ireland on your right and up the pedestrian Grafton Street to St Stephen's Green. The two cathedrals of St Patrick's and Christ Church are to the west of Trinity College, as is Dublin Castle. The political district surrounds An Dáil (Parliament) which is to the east of Grafton Street. This is also where the main Georgian part of the city remains intact and where the National Museum and National Gallery are situated. The inner city, as it is known, is bounded on the north by the Royal Canal and on the south by the Grand Canal. To the west of the city is the Phoenix Park, the largest enclosed urban park in Europe.

Population and People

Dublin has grown rapidly since the foundation of the State, principally because of its importance as an intellectual and administrative centre. The population of the built-up area of the city increased from 419,000 in 1926 to over 1 million in 1986. The statistical result of this growth is that Dublin's current population of 1,070,429 now accounts for 29% of the State's entire population. In the early 1980s more than half of the city's population was under 25, and although the number of births is declining every year, Dublin will remain for the foreseeable future a very young city. Twenty five per cent of the city's current population is still of school-going age.

The city has always been a melting pot, attracting to this day native Irish from rural areas in search of employment, attracting in the past foreign invaders who intermarried and settled, and today attracting more and more people from around the globe in search of a relationship with, and an understanding of, the city, its people and its culture. Many of these latter-day immigrants arrive to take up positions of employment in the many vibrant areas of the Irish economy.

Dublin's Economy

Traditional inner-city and port-related industries have been in decline since the late 1960s. Most of Dublin's industry is today situated on peripheral industrial estates. Much of that industry is foreign-owned, a result of the policies of successive Governments over the past twenty-five years. The idea was, and still is to a great extent, to attract foreign investment by offering tax incentive packages to international companies on the look-out for set-up locations. Representatives of the semi-state Industrial Development Authority (IDA), now disbanded and reconstituted under different names, successfully argued over the years that Ireland offers an educated workforce, an attractive environment and a stepping stone to a market of over 300 million in the European Union.

Dublin is, like many modern cities, a thriving mix of service industries, traditional manufacturers such as Guinness, W&R Jacob and the Smurfit Group, as well as the newer firms in electronics, software, pharmaceuticals, chemicals and other growth sectors. Dublin's leading business sectors are Automotive and Engineering, Software, Computers and Electronics, Food and Drink, Avionics, Pharmaceuticals, Printing and Paper, and Financial Services. Tourism provides a substantial number of jobs and although some of this is seasonal, Dublin is less affected by this seasonality on account of the number and variety of visitors the capital attracts throughout the year.

Being the centre of Government, Dublin, through Government Civil Service administration jobs and the various semi-State organisations and Corporation and Council departments, is a huge white-collar employment area. Government policy is now directed at beginning the necessary steps towards greater decentralisation of Government employees, thus assisting the emergency renewal of rural communities, rapidly dying through a decline in the numbers of family farms and the result of continuous years of emigration.

Government and Politics

The Republic of Ireland is a parliamentary democracy and Dublin is the centre of Government. The Lower House (Dáil Éireann) and the Upper House (Seanad) both sit in Leinster House on Kildare Street. There are 166 members (TDs) of Dáil Éireann. At time of writing there is a centre-right Government coalition, led by Fianna Fáil (Soldiers of Destiny) and supported by the Progressive Democrats. The other principal political parties are Fine Gael (Tribe of the Gaels) and the Labour Party. Two smaller parties - the Green Party and Sinn Féin - together with independent TDs, make up about 10% of the national vote. Irish people are keenly interested in politics, following political events closely through the print and broadcast media.

The President of Ireland is Mary McAleese, elected by the Irish people in November 1997 for the traditional seven-year term. The office of the President is largely symbolic, carrying few constitutional powers. The symbolic importance of the Presidency was given an enormous boost during Mary Robinson's seven-year term (1990-97) and this shift in emphasis has continued under President McAleese's presidency.

Religion

The Catholic Church remains a powerful and influential institution in Ireland today, though they would be the first to admit that their moral authority is not as universally accepted as it was in times past. And, while the majority of Irish people declare themselves Catholic, in Dublin that majority is receding as a young, outward-looking population comes in increasing contact with international cultural influences. The Protestant community in the Republic is relatively influential for its size - Protestants make up approximately 4% of the population - and in the Dublin cathedrals of St Patrick and Christ Church they have two of the finest religious buildings on the entire island.

Language

Irish is a Celtic language and is closely related to the Gaelic languages of Scotland, Wales and Brittany in France. An estimated 83,000 people who live in Gaeltacht areas of Ireland (areas, especially in the west of the country, in which Irish Gaelic is the designated language) use it as their first language. Elsewhere, Irish is spoken by some, understood by many, but seldom practised on a daily basis. In Dublin, a new, independent radio station, Raidió na Life (Liffey Radio) was launched in 1993 in response to the growing demand in the capital by Irish-language speakers for their own station. A few years later, Telefís na Gaeilge (TnaG), a national television station, broadcasting exclusively in Irish and making many of its own programmes, was launched and seems to be surviving in an increasingly commercial broadcasting environment. Despite, then, the predictions over the past twenty-five years that Irish is a dying language, it seems that the revival in interest, among young people in particular, many of them in Dublin, will guarantee its survival as a living, minority European language.

Arts and Culture

Literature

Three Dublin writers have won the Nobel Prize for Literature: William Butler Yeats, George Bernard Shaw and Samuel Beckett. It comes as a surprise to some that James Joyce is not on that list. Joyce is a towering figure in Irish literature, a significant achievement when one considers other Irish writers before and after him: Jonathan Swift, Oliver Goldsmith, Oscar Wilde, Seán O'Casey, John Millington Synge, Patrick Kavanagh, and of course Yeats, Shaw and Beckett.

James Joyce (1882-1941) was always a Dublin writer, even though all his writing was created after he had left the city for good. His famous novel, *Ulysses*, is one of the most widely-read works of fiction in the 20th century, and his other works, notably his collection of short stories, *Dubliners*, his autobiography, *A Portrait of the Artist as a Young Man*, and the unique experiment with language in *Finnegans Wake*, together make up a body of work that is unequalled in Irish literature. Joyce was born in Dublin in 1882 and attended the Catholic University in Newman House on St Stephen's Green. When he was 22 he met Nora Barnacle, a Galway woman who was working as a chambermaid in a Dublin hotel. Four months later they were on their way to the Continent

James Joyce (1882-1941).

where they were to spend the rest of their lives, living for periods in Trieste, Zurich, Rome and Paris. Joyce, a man of culture and sharp intellect, was very critical of Ireland from a distance, a country he saw as being in the stranglehold of the Catholic Church. Yet he wrote about his native city with marvellous perception and genuine affection. On 16 June in Dublin every year, Bloomsday (named after the hero of *Ulysses*, Leopold Bloom) celebrations smother the city as thousands of Joycean scholars and enthusiasts flock to the capital to take part in a day of readings, tours, street-theatre, and plenty of eating and drinking in and around some of the places associated with the famous novel.

Jonathan Swift (1667-1745) was born and educated in Dublin, and returned after many adult years in England to take up the Deanship of St Patrick's Cathedral in 1713. His satirical writings criticising the English Government over their discriminatory and uncompromising policies in Ireland made him a much trusted and highly-regarded figure among the downtrodden classes of Dublin. His most famous book, the satirical *Gulliver's Travels*, was written in 1726 and remains to this day a children's classic.

Oliver Goldsmith (1728-74), poet and dramatist who was educated in Trinity College, wrote *The Vicar of Wakefield*, *She Stoops to Conquer*, and his famous and evocative poem, *The Deserted Village*. You can see his statue outside the main entrance to Trinity College.

Bram Stoker (1847-1912) was born at Marino Crescent in north Dublin and became unexpectedly famous through his fictional creation, *Dracula*. The novel stands on its own as a masterpiece of Gothic horror with psychological undertones, and reading it now one can easily understand what attracted film directors to the story.

William Butler Yeats (1865-1939) was born in Sandymount in south Dublin. By the time of his death he had become an internationally recognised poet, having won the Nobel Prize in 1923. His interests were in Irish mythology and nationalist literature, and he was instrumental in setting the Irish literary revival on the road. He helped to found the Abbey Theatre in 1904 and his play, *On Baile's Strand*, was the first to be performed there. He was appointed to the Senate for six years of the Irish Free State Government. A Henry Moore sculpture depicting the poet can be found in St Stephen's Green.

Oscar Wilde (1854-1900) was born at No. 21 Westland Row and spent much of his formative years in the Wilde home at No. 1 Merrion Square. Following his studies at Trinity College he left for London where he quickly became the toast of London society, enjoying his reputation as London's leading drawing-room conversationalist. His plays appeared first on London stages where they were hugely successful, among them *The Importance of Being Earnest*, *Lady Windermere's Fan* and *A Woman of No Importance*. He was later to become tragically embroiled in a court case which publicised his homosexuality and shocked a society he had earlier so engagingly captured. He was sentenced to two years in prison where he wrote the moving poem, *Ballad of Reading Gaol*. He died in Paris in a lonely hotel room, abandoned by a society which not long before had taken him to their hearts. You can see a plaque on the house in which he was born and also at No. 1 Merrion Square where he lived with his father, Sir William Wilde and his mother, Lady Constance Wilde ('Speranza').

Oscar Wilde (1854-1900).

George Bernard Shaw (1856-1950) was born in Synge Street, near a stretch of the Grand Canal. He left school when he was fifteen and moved to London in his early twenties. He wrote prolifically, and not just drama, for he had a keen interest in the affairs of both the Irish and the English nations. Among his best-known plays are *Arms and the Man*, *John Bull's Other Island*, *Pygmalion (My Fair Lady)* and *Saint Joan*. He received the Nobel Prize in 1925. During his lifetime he championed many causes and was an outspoken critic of people and politics with which he did not agree. He was a practicising and campaigning vegetarian for all of his long and active adult life. A bronze statue stands inside the National Gallery in recognition of the importance of his patronage of that institution. His birthplace at No. 33 Synge Street was recently opened to the public as a Shaw museum.

Samuel Beckett (1906-89) was born in Foxrock, a fashionable suburb on the south of Dublin. He studied French in Trinity College and lectured in that subject in Trinity from 1930 to 1932. When he arrived in Paris he worked with Joyce for a time as his secretary. During the Second World War he was involved in the French Resistance. His play, *Waiting for Godot*, catapulted him onto the international literary stage with its stark, original and ultimately pessimistic view of the world, relieved by the terse but genuine comedy in the writing. Beckett always wrote in French and translated his works into English. He was awarded the Nobel Prize for Literature in 1969.

Samuel Beckett (1906-89).

Other Dublin writers of note are **Flann O'Brien** (1912-66), best remembered for his comic classics, *The Third Policeman* and *At Swim-two-birds*, but also for his regular satirical writings in the *Irish Times* under the pseudonym Myles na Gopaleen. He wrote in both languages, Irish and English; **Brendan Behan** (1923-64), who literally drank himself to an early death, managing, before that tragic yet inevitable event, to write powerful plays about life in prison and the IRA; **J.M. Synge** (1871-1909), whose evocative and linguistically powerful depiction of life on the Aran Islands in his famous play, *The Playboy of the Western World*, caused riots in the Abbey Theatre in 1907; **Seán O'Casey** (1880-1964), a working-class writer who wrote three classic Irish plays, *Shadow of a Gunman*, *Juno and the Paycock* and *The Plough and the Stars*. O'Casey's plays caused riots on their opening nights, none more so than *'Plough'* which many in the audience misinterpreted as being an insult to the heroes of the 1916 Rising; **Patrick Kavanagh** (1906-67), born in County Monaghan but who adopted Dublin city in his adult years. After Yeats, regarded by many as Ireland's greatest poet.

Dublin literature is alive and well and still producing writers of international stature: **Roddy Doyle**, novelist, won the prestigious Booker Prize in 1993 with *Paddy Clarke Ha Ha Ha*, the novel reaching the number one position in the American bestseller list early in 1994; **John Banville**, novelist, was born in Wexford but now lives in Dublin. His unusual books on Copernicus, Kepler and Newton, as well as his Booker nomination *The Book of Evidence* have placed him among Ireland's finest living writers; **Seamus Heaney**, poet, was born in County Derry but now lives in Dublin. An outstanding writer, he won the Nobel Prize for Literature in 1995; **Neil Jordan** is a novelist and short-story writer and internationally renowned film director. His films include *Mona Lisa* and the award-winning *Crying Game*; **Brendan Kennelly**, poet, was born in Listowel in County Kerry but lives in Dublin and is Professor of English Studies in Trinity College; and **Christopher Nolan**, whose *Damburst of Dreams* and *Under the Eye of the Clock* catapulted this severely disabled young writer into the literary limelight. Without a shadow of a doubt, Dublin's remarkable literary tradition lives on.

Music

Irish traditional music is at the heart of the music scene in Ireland, and Dublin, being the centre of so many cultural activities, could arguably be described as the current centre of traditional music. All except the most successful traditional musicians have to earn their bread and butter in more conventional ways - as computer operators, teachers, civil servants, nurses (in fact, name the profession and it's a sure bet you'll find traditional musicians among their ranks). Most conventional employment is in Dublin and it is in the pubs of the great metropolis that you will find musicians from all corners of the country playing the distinctive styles of their regions.

The place to hear live traditional music in Dublin is in the pubs (see *A Tour of Dublin Pubs* and *Entertainment* in this Guide). Throughout the year dedicated musicians gather in certain pubs around Dublin and play jigs, reels, hornpipes, polkas and slow airs in a *seisiún* (the Irish word for a jamming session). The most commonly played instruments in traditional Irish music are the uilleann

Live traditional music in the pubs.
Photo: Temple Bar Properties.

pipes, the fiddle, the flute, the tin whistle, the box accordion, the concertina, the bodhrán, the guitar, the banjo, the mandolin, the bouzouki and the piano. While in Dublin you may be lucky to come across a 'céili', where people will gather to dance Irish 'sets' to the melody and time of live traditional music. In recent times, there has been a revival of set dancing and it is now possible to learn how to dance a set or two at a number of teaching workshops in Dublin throughout the year.

Ireland is famous for its outstanding musicians, be they traditional or rock artists. Some of the following, although not necessarily born in Dublin, spend most of their time in the capital. Without doubt, the most internationally well-known are Dublin-born **U2** (Bono, The Edge, Adam Clayton, Larry Mullen), and close on their heels are **Sinead O'Connor**, **The Chieftains, The Dubliners, Chris de Burgh, Boyzone, Christy Moore** and **Enya**. **Bob Geldof** is perhaps more famous for his pioneering live concert charity work in aid of the starving victims of the 1984 Ethiopian Famine than as a singer/songwriter with the Boomtown Rats. As a result of the success of U2, the contemporary music scene in Dublin has developed rapidly and the city is now bubbling with a creative music energy that many young, budding bands have latched onto. On the live concert front, **The Point** is a popular venue which attracts some of the biggest and best live acts in the world, while the **National Concert Hall** is the premier venue for classical concerts and recitals.

Film

In the last decade the Irish film industry has come out of the shadows, establishing itself as an influential force in world cinema. Many Irish-made films have been international successes, among them *The Commitments*, a film about young Dublin musicians almost hitting the big time. Adapted from a book by Roddy Doyle and directed by Alan Parker, it captured the wit and repartee of some of the north Dublin suburbs.

My Left Foot, starring Daniel Day Lewis, was a huge international success. Day Lewis won an Oscar for his portrayal of the severely handicapped real-life figure, Christy Brown. The Irish director of *My Left Foot,* Jim Sheridan, successfully adapted a powerful John B. Keane play, *The Field*, starring Richard Harris in the lead role. In the mid nineties, another Sheridan film attracted much attention from critics and filmgoers alike. *In The Name Of The Father* depicts the experience of Gerry Conlon (Day Lewis), one of the Guildford Four, all of whom were wrongly convicted of an IRA bombing in Guildford, England in 1974 and who spent 16 years in British jails before being released following the overturning of their original conviction.

Neil Jordan is another Dubliner who has established himself among the leading directors of the day. His *Mona Lisa, The Crying Game, Michael Collins* and, more recently, *The Butcher Boy*, have won him many plaudits, establishing him as a force in world cinema. John Huston's last film before he died was an adaptation of one of James Joyce's most famous short stories, *The Dead*. The film is marvellously true to the story and any admirer of Dublin or of Joyce should see it. Dublin-born Gabriel Byrne has become one of Hollywood's leading men, and his film, *Into the West*, was a delightful and seductive tale of two young Dublin 'travellers' (travelling people) literally riding out of trouble on a white horse and across the midlands to the west coast, pursued by well-wishers and evil-doers. Two films released in 1998 dealt with distinctly different topics. *The General,* directed by John Boorman, who lives in Ireland, tells the story of Dublin gangster Martin Cahill who was shot dead in broad daylight on a Dublin street a few years back. It stars Brendan Gleeson. *Dancing at Lughnasa,* by contrast, is a thought-provoking, rural film, set in County Donegal in the fifties and relating the story of five orphaned sisters and their struggle for survival. Directed by Pat O'Connor and starring Meryl Streep, it is adapted from Irish playwright Brian Friel's award-winning play of the same name.

Art

Ireland has never produced a painter of true genius who stands, like Joyce in another artistic medium, head and shoulders above almost everyone else. That said, there has always been a tradition of excellent Irish painters, and none more visually original and powerful than Dublin-born **Jack B. Yeats** (1871-1957), brother of W.B. The Yeats' father, **John Butler Yeats**, was also a fine painter. The National Gallery of Ireland on Dublin's Merrion Square houses a fine collection of Irish and international paintings, including a room devoted to Yeats. Two other major art galleries are the Hugh Lane Municipal Gallery of Modern Art on Parnell Square and the Irish Museum of Modern Art in the former Royal Hospital in Kilmainham.

Architecture

The first Dublin churches were built in wood and daub. These were replaced by stone structures, but few have survived from the Middle Ages. The Protestant *St Audoen's Church* on High Street is one of Dublin's oldest churches, there being some dispute regarding its age. The general consensus is that the ruins are of an Anglo-Norman church built in 1169. Dublin's oldest building is the crypt of *Christ Church Cathedral* which dates to its foundation in 1172. Both Protestant cathedrals, Christ Church and *St Patrick's*, are early-Gothic in style and what one sees today are two heavily restored edifices.

The first great classical building in Ireland was Dublin's *Royal Hospital,* Kilmainham, built in 1684 and modelled on Les Invalides in Paris. It was recently restored and now houses the Irish Museum of Modern Art. The 18th-century saw the Protestant ascendancy build elegant houses and magnificent public buildings in a period during which Dublin's physical shape and internal make-up changed dramatically. The building renaissance began with *Parliament House* on College Green (1729). When built, it was the largest

Trinity College.   Photo: Peter Zoeller.

Palladian public building in the British Isles. Even today it stands colossus-like in the centre of the modern city. It now houses the *Bank of Ireland*. The two principal public buildings belonging to the Georgian period are the *Custom House* (1791) and the *Four Courts* (1802), both overlooking the River Liffey and both the work of arguably Dublin's greatest architect, **James Gandon**. Born and educated in England, he was invited to design public buildings in St Petersburg, but he decided to come to Dublin where his architectural legacy is immense. Some other important architects of the Georgian period were **Thomas Cooley** (*the Royal Exchange*); the German-born **Richard Cassels**, later changed to **Castle** when he married and settled in Ireland (*Iveagh House* and *Newman House* on St Stephen's Green, *Leinster House* on Kildare Street, and the *Rotunda Hospital* on Parnell Square); **William Chambers** (*Trinity College Chapel* and *Examination Hall*, *Charlemont House* on Parnell Square, and the remarkable *Casino* at Marino, 3 miles from the centre of the city to the north).

Many of the most influential architects were English-born (one of them, William Chambers, never actually came to Dublin to oversee his buildings being constructed). A feature of the Georgian period was the superb craftsmanship of stucco workers, stone-carvers, wood-carvers, painters, glassmakers, silversmiths and other craftsmen. The plasterwork on many walls and ceilings of domestic houses is quite exquisite, and the work on many of the larger houses and mansions is simply breathtaking. It can be quite difficult to get inside these buildings nowadays, but the tourist office on Suffolk Street will give you a list of those which are open to the public. Also, see *Things To See And Do* in this Guide.

After the Georgian period Dublin architecture came under the influence of the Victorian style of building design, using similar materials as those in the 18th century - brick, stone, slate and ironwork. A walk along Baggot Street out to the inner southern suburb of Ballsbridge is an interesting way to see the difference between the two periods, as the district around Ballsbridge was developed from the 1830s onwards. Modern Dublin architecture does not have a distinctive style. The city has, in fact, developed in the 1900s without the foundations of an architectural vision. This is why, today, the visitor's eye is invariably drawn towards not only the magnificent public buildings of the 18th century, but also by the pleasing uniformity of the Georgian squares.

Getting To And Around Dublin

Getting To Dublin

By Air
Dublin Airport is a busy, international airport with flights arriving from and departing to many international airports around the world.
From Britain **Aer Lingus**, the Irish national airline (tel: 01 8444777), is the main carrier and flies from ten airports into Dublin (London Heathrow, London Stansted, Birmingham, Bristol, Edinburgh, Glasgow, Jersey, Leeds/Bradford, Manchester, Newcastle). In the high season there can be as many as twenty-three daily Aer Lingus Dublin-London Heathrow flights operating, in addition to the numerous other carriers (Ryanair, British Midlands, CityJet) which between them service Heathrow, Gatwick, Stansted, Luton, London City Airport, East Midlands, Glasgow, Newcastle, Leeds/Bradford, Manchester, Liverpool, Birmingham, Bristol, Cardiff and Bournemouth.
From North America Flights from North America directly into Dublin are on the increase. Aer Lingus remains the chief supplier, with flights from New York (JFK and Newark), Boston, Chicago and Los Angeles. Delta have a daily flight from New York to Dublin, while American Trans Air fly from New York, Chicago and Los Angeles.
From Europe The competition within Europe is also hotting up and is likely to change from year to year. Currently, Aer Lingus operates direct flights to Dublin from Amsterdam, Brussels, Copenhagen, Dusseldorf, Frankfurt, Milan, Paris, Rome, Stockholm and Zurich. CityJet flies directly from Paris, Malaga and Faro (Portugal) into Dublin. Ryanair flies directly into Dublin from Paris and Brussels.
Contact your local travel agent for details on all flights.

By Sea
Regular ferry crossings between Holyhead and Dublin and Holyhead and Dun Laoghaire ensure a constant flow of foot-passenger, car, coach and heavy transport traffic in and out of Dublin every day.
Irish Ferries (tel: 01-6610511) operates the Holyhead-Dublin Port crossing. The sailing time is around $3^1/_2$ hours. Irish Ferries also sail between Pembroke and Rosslare.

Stena Sealink (tel: 01-2047700) operates the relatively new, high-speed ferry, the Stena Explorer, between Holyhead and Dun Laoghaire. The journey time is about $1^1/_2$ hours, but bad weather can affect sailings quite frequently. Stena also sail between Holyhead and Dublin Port (car ferry), between Fishguard and Rosslare, and between Stranraer and Larne.
Swansea Ferries (tel: 021-271166) sail from Swansea to Cork. **Merchant Ferries** (tel: 01-8551551) sail from Liverpool to Dublin (commenced service in February 1999).
Isle of Man Steam Packaging Company (tel: 44-990-523523) operate daily the Sea Cat high-speed ferry between Liverpool and Dublin Port. From France, **Irish Ferries** and **Brittany Ferries** operate regular sailings to Ireland. Irish Ferries sail from Cherbourg and from Roscoff (summer only) to Rosslare. **Brittany Ferries** (tel: 021-277801) sail from Roscoff to Cork. There are regular buses from cities in Britain to Dublin via the Holyhead ferries. The bus journey from London to Dublin takes about 13 hours. Telephone the Irish Tourist Board in London (tel: 0171-4933201) for information on this service.

Getting Around Dublin

To and from Dublin Airport
Dublin Bus operates a fare-paying bus service between Dublin Airport and the central bus station, Busarus (tel: 01-8366111), 7 days a week. Between Monday and Saturday buses run every fifteen minutes, starting at 06.45 with the last bus leaving before 23.00. On

Sundays the buses run every 20-30 minutes and less frequently after 20.00 hours. Some of the buses travel to Heuston (train) Station. Journey time for these special express airport buses is about 30 minutes and the adult fare is £3 (£3.50 to Heuston). Dublin Bus also operate a commuter bus, the 41/41C, which runs between Eden Quay in the city centre and the airport at regular intervals. This bus stops at commuter pick-up and drop-off points along its route and the journey time as a result is about 45 minutes. However, the fare is only £1.20 and it has slightly longer operating hours.

To and from the Ferry Terminals

The Holyhead-Dublin Ferryport Ferry is serviced by buses between Busarus (tel: 01-8366111) and the Dublin Ferryport Terminal. To get to Dun Laoghaire Ferryport, catch the 46A commuter bus in the city centre, or take the rapid-rail commuter train, DART, from Pearse, Connolly or Tara Street Stations.

Around Dublin by Bus

Dublin Bus routes around Dublin are extensive. You can call in to their 59 O'Connell Street office (tel: 01-8734222 or 8366111) and pick up all information

Dublin's Rapid Transit Rail System - DART

on routes, fares and the numerous discount fares and multi-journey tickets available. Last buses leave the city centre around 23.30, but on Friday and Saturday nights late buses depart from College, Westmoreland and D'Olier Streets to the suburbs, running till as late as 03.00 for a flat fee of £2.50. If you see *An Lár* on the front of a bus it means its destination is the city centre.

Around Dublin by Train

DART, the rapid-rail commuter train, currently operates only along the coast. There are plans to construct a light rail network to other suburbs over the next five years. The trip from Howth peninsula on the northside, through the city centre and all the way to Bray in County Wicklow is a journey well worth doing. Some of the views of Dublin Bay along the route are quite spectacular. Dublin city DART stations are at Connolly Station, Tara Street Station and Pearse Station (Westland Row), and there are twenty-two suburban stations between Howth and Bray. Fares are reasonable and there are numerous discount fares available. Enquire at **Iarnród Éireann**, 35 Abbey Street Lower (tel: 01-8366222).

Taxis

There are metered taxis at the mainline railway stations, the ferryports and Dublin Airport, and also at taxi ranks around the city. You can also flag them down - though this is not as easy as in some European and American cities - or you can phone for one from your hotel room. Whichever method you use, your taxi will not be cheap, so be prepared. A typical single fare from the city centre to Dublin Airport will cost about £15.

Driving/Car Rental

Driving in Ireland is on the left in right-hand-drive cars. Rush-hour traffic in Dublin is particularly heavy, even worse than many, more populated, European cities. There are parking meters (20p/50p/£1 coins) on most streets and an increasing number of multi-level and surface car parks. No matter where you park, never leave anything on view in the car. Renting a car in Dublin is only a problem during July and August when it really can be impossible to get hold of one. It is always better to book in advance. Bord Fáilte publishes an information sheet which lists the companies who are members of the Car Rental Council (tel: 01-6761690) and who will guarantee a quality service. Below is a list of some of the main car rental companies:
Avis Rent-a-Car, Dublin Airport, Arrivals Hall (tel: 01-6057500)
Budget Rent-a-Car, Dublin Airport (tel: 01-8445150)
Dan Dooley Car & Van Rentals, 42/43 Westland Row, D2 (tel: 01-6772723)

Hertz Rent-a-Car, Dublin Airport (tel: 01-8445466) and Leeson Street Upper, D2 (tel: 01-6767476)
Murray's Europcar Rent-a-Car, Baggot Street Bridge, D2 (tel: 01-6142888)
Windsor Car Rentals, Dublin Airport (tel: 01-8400800)

Bicycle Hire
Cycling can be somewhat hazardous in a city dominated by the car and with a limited supply of dedicated cycleways. Nonetheless, it's still the best way to get around – if you dare. Day hire should be in the region of £7-8, while a week in the saddle will set you back £30 upwards. You can rent a bike from:
Dublin Bike Tours (city centre) (tel: 01-6790899). They also organise guided tours of the city by bike.
The Bike Shop UCD, Belfield, D4 (tel: (01-2600749).
Rent-a-Bike, 58 Lower Gardiner Street, D1 (tel: 01-8725399).
McDonald's Cycles, 38 Wexford Street, D2 (tel: 01-4752586).
Track Cycles, 8 Botanic Road, Glasnevin (tel: 01-8500252).
Joe Daly's, Main Street, Dundrum, tel: (01-2981485).

Tours
Bus Tours
A number of bus companies operate regular tours of the city during the summer months. **Dublin Bus** run a 2³/₄ hour tour in an open-top double-decker bus throughout the year at 10.15 and 14.15 daily. The tour costs £8. Dublin Bus also run a daily tour called *Coast and Castle Tour* which travels via Howth and Malahide (price £12), and a *South Coast Tour* which travels daily along the south coast returning via Enniskerry (price £12). The *Hop On Hop Off* is a continuous open-top bus which does a tour of the city throughout the day and which stops to let people on and off at different tourist locations. A ticket allows you to use this bus all day and costs £6. Tours can be booked at the Dublin Bus office, 59 O'Connell Street (tel: 01-7033028) or at the Tourist Office on Suffolk Street.
Gray Line operate a Dublin city tour during the summer months and tickets and information can be obtained at their desk in Dublin Tourism, Suffolk Street (tel: 01-6057705). There is a variety of morning and afternoon tours and several day-long tours outside Dublin.

Gray Line also organise tours to Jury's Irish Cabaret and to Doyle's Irish Cabaret in the evening.
Bus Éireann operate seven-day tours out of the city, among them the popular *Wicklow/Glendalough Tour* which operates between April and October and costs £17 (adults) and £9 (children), and *The Boyne Valley/Newgrange Tour* which operates between May and September and costs £17 (adults) and £9 (children). Tickets and information on all tours can be obtained at the Tourist Office on Suffolk Street, at the Bus Éireann office on O'Connell Street, or at Busarus (tel: 01-8366111).

Walking Tours
If you intend spending several days walking around the city, you might be tempted to buy a copy of *Stroller's Guide to Dublin*, a book of fifteen walking tours of the inner city by the author of this pocket guide. Below is a list of the main, organised

Dublin Bus Sightseeing Tours.   Photo: Peter Zoeller.

walking tours of the city:
Trinity Tours operate from Front Square and during the summer depart every 15-20 minutes. The tour of Trinity College includes entrance to the Book of Kells.
Dublin Footsteps have been operating tours from Bewley's Oriental Café on Grafton Street since 1987. Tours include *Georgian Dublin, Medieval Dublin, Literary Dublin* (tel: 01-4960641).
Historical Walking Tours operate regular tours from the front gates of Trinity College and usually head towards Christ Church Cathedral, stopping at various places en route (tel: 01-8780227).

Well-known Dublin historian and author of numerous books on Dublin, **Éamonn MacThomáis** can be found at the Bank of Ireland on College Green every Tuesday throughout the year, from where he takes three tours over the course of the day, including a guided tour of the House of Lords (tel: 01-6711488).

James Joyce's nephew, Ken Monaghan, organises **James Joyce Literary Tours** from the James Joyce Cultural Centre, 35 North Great George's Street, D1 (tel: 01-8731984).

Old Dublin Tours operate a tour of medieval Dublin from the main gates of Christ Church Cathedral (tel: 01-4533423).

Temple Bar Walking Tours operate daily at 12.00 and 14.00 from outside the ESB building on Fleet Street. Tours cost £6 (adult), £5 (concessions) (tel: 01-6725096).

The 1916 Rebellion Tour starts from the International Bar on Wicklow Street at 11.30, Tuesday to Saturday. Tours cost £6 (adults), £5 (concessions) (tel: 01-6762493).

Walk Macabre is, according to the blurb, a 'unique evening of murder, the supernatural and the bizarre'. Tours operate Monday to Friday at 19.30 hours and booking is essential. Contact the ticket desk at Dublin Tourism (tel: 01-6057769). Visit the scenes of great escapes, murders and mythical happenings with **The Zozimus Experience.** Tours start at nightfall from the pedestrian gate of Dublin Castle opposite the Olympia Theatre. Booking is essential and tours cost £6. (tel: 01-6618646)

A Traditional Irish Music Pub Crawl takes place every night between

Horse Drawn Carriages at St Stephen's Green. Photo: Peter Zoeller.

May and October, starting from the Oliver St John Gogarty pub in Temple Bar, cost £6. (tel: 01-4780191).

The Jameson Literary Pub Crawl is a popular evening tour of some of Dublin's 'literary' pubs. It starts at 19.30 from The Duke Pub on Duke Street (off Grafton Street) and visits a number of pubs during the tour. The two actor/guides perform extracts from Dublin plays, novels and poems. Tours are nightly between May and September and cost £6 (adults) and £5 (students). (tel: 01-4540228). There's an additional tour on Sundays at noon.

Finally, **Audio Walking Tour of Dublin** (7 Aston Quay) provides you with a pre-recorded tour of the city. Simply hire the portable equipment and away you go (tel: 01-6705266 or 8324734). Cost: half day £6, full day £8.

Getting Around Ireland

By Train

Irish Rail (Iarnród Éireann) operates regular train services to mainline stations throughout Ireland from Heuston and Connolly Stations, the main train stations in Dublin city. There are many discount fares available; for example, an *Irish Explorer Rail Only* ticket allows one adult five days unlimited travel in the Republic of Ireland for £67. The Iarnród Éireann Travel Centre, 35 Abbey Street Lower (tel: 01-8366222) is the place to make all enquiries.

By Bus

Irish Bus (Bus Éireann) has a nationwide network of buses serving all the major cities and most towns and villages outside the Dublin area. **Dublin Bus (Bus Átha Cliath)** controls all public bus services in the greater Dublin area, including parts of Wicklow, Meath and Kildare. There are many discount fares available; for example, an *Irish Rambler Bus Only* ticket allows one adult three days' unlimited travel in the Republic of Ireland for £28, and eight days for £68. An *Emerald Card Bus/Rail* ticket allows one adult eight days' unlimited bus and train travel <u>throughout all Ireland</u> for £115 (children's rate is £58). The telephone number of Bus Éireann is (01-8366111), and of Dublin Bus (01-8734222).

Essential Visitor Information

Customs

The long tradition of duty-free shopping within Europe is under severe threat in the corridors of power in Brussels and Strasbourg, but at time of writing it looks as if it will get a brief reprieve before final abolition in the early years of the millennium. Duty-free shopping at Dublin Airport is relaxed - if you are not dashing for your plane - and competitively priced. You can purchase duty-free alcohol, tobacco, clothes, perfume, confectionery, camera and hi-fi equipment and much more. Duty-free goods are also available on the main ferry routes into the country.

Money and Banks

The unit of currency is the Irish Punt. At time of writing the Irish Punt and the Pound Sterling are almost on par. One Irish Punt (£1) is made up of 100 pence. Coins come in 1p, 2p, 5p, 10p, 20p, 50p, £1. Notes are in £5, £10, £20, £50, £100 denominations.

The best place to change your money is in one of the main banks or in the international bureaux de change. Dublin banks open Monday to Friday between 10.00 and 15.00. Some banks open till 16.00. Smaller banks close between 12.30 and 13.30, but this age-old practice is disappearing due to the increased competition from other financial institutions which open through lunch. Many banks stay open till 17.00 on Thursdays. The bureau de change at Dublin Airport is open much longer hours than normal banks. Look out for the one at the baggage collection as it's a handy place to change your money before the usual stresses of arriving in a new place occupy your thoughts. All major credit cards are widely accepted around Dublin and you can usually get cash on Visa and Access from a bank or from the cash-point machines outside the main banks.

Cost of Living

A direct result of Ireland's emergence as a strong economy with one of the most healthy balance sheets in Europe is its parallel rise in the cost of living. Nowhere is this rise more tangible than in Dublin, where house prices and almost every other price soared throughout the second half of the nineties. Visitors to Dublin will see their money disappearing in Dublin's shops at least as quickly as it would were they doing a bit of shopping in London or Paris. Below is a random list of some typical Dublin prices. As in any city, they can vary from place to place:

A pint of beer	£2.20
A measure of whiskey	£2.00
20 cigarettes	£3.00
A litre of milk	75p
A glass of fresh juice	£2.00
A cup of coffee/tea	£1.00p
Daily newspapers	85p
A sandwich/roll	£2.00
5 km bus ride	£1.10
A roll of film (24)	£4.50
Popular music cassette	£9.00

Average new three-bedroomed house in the Dublin region £130,000

Everything you buy has some kind of consumer tax included in the price. You can claim back the Value-Added Tax (VAT) element in the price for any goods you are taking out of the EU with you. VAT can be as high as 21% on many items. Most of the large stores will deduct the VAT at time of purchase if you tell the counter staff that you are from outside the EU. Many stores will issue you with a **Tax-Free Voucher** that can be refunded at Dublin or Shannon Airports. If you are leaving Ireland by ferry the Tax-Free Voucher will be stamped by Customs and when you get home you post them back to Ireland to get your refund. Over 2,000 stores in Ireland participate in the Tax-Free scheme.

Tipping is less of a custom than it is in some countries. Nevertheless, there are occasions when a tip is recommended. Most restaurants add their own service charge to your bill - this can be as high as 15% - so there is no need to tip unless you want to show your gratitude for individual attention. When a service charge is not included in the bill it is considered generous to leave 10% on top of the total bill, however it really is at your discretion. It is normal to tip hotel porters 50p per bag. As for taxis, 10% is considered generous, though it is again at your discretion. It is not normal to tip in pubs, though if you are served at table in the lounge you can tip if you wish.

Some Embassies

American: 42 Elgin Road, Ballsbridge, D4. Tel: 01-6688777
Australian: 2nd Floor, Fitzwilton House, Wilton Terrace, D2. Tel: 01-6761517
British: 31/33 Merrion Road, D4. Tel: 01-2053700
Canadian: 4th Floor, 65/68 St Stephen's Green, D2. Tel: 01-4781988
French: 36 Ailesbury Road, D4. Tel: 01-2601666
German: 31 Trimleston Avenue,

Booterstown, Co. Dublin.
Tel: 01-2693011
Italian: 63/65 Northumberland Road,
Ballsbridge, D4. Tel: 01-6601744
Japanese: Nutley Building, Merrion
Centre, Nutley Lane, D4.
Tel: 01-2694244
Spanish: 17A Merlyn Park, Ballsbridge,
D4. Tel: 01-2691640
Swiss: 6 Ailesbury Road, D4.
Tel: 01-2692515

Tourist Offices
Bord Fáilte - Irish Tourist Board,
Head Office, Baggot Street Bridge, D2.
Tel: 01-6024000
Dublin Tourism have their office at
Suffolk Street, Dublin 2.
Tel: 1850 230330.
From outside Ireland: 00-353-
669792083

Telephones
Telecom Éireann has until recently held a
monopoly on providing a telephone
service to Irish consumers. However,
European law dictates that monopolies
are a thing of the past, so Telecom are
preparing to enter the competitive
environment. This will probably improve
an already efficient telephone system
available throughout the country. To call
abroad from Dublin, dial the
international code 00, then your own
country code, followed by your area
code (drop the first 0 if there is one) and
then your number. It is considerably
cheaper to make calls between 18.00
and 08.00 Monday to Friday, and at
weekends, particularly Sunday.
Phonecards are becoming the standard
method of using public phones. These
can be bought in most newsagents and
in all post offices. You cannot make
operator-assisted international calls
using a Phonecard. If you are in trouble,
dial 10 for operator assistance. The
International Operator is 114.

Email
An number of cybercafés have recently
opened throughout the city. You can
drop in and email your family and
friends to tell them what a wonderful
time you are having in Dublin.
Try: Cyberia Café, Temple Lane, D2
(tel: 01-6797607);
Global Internet Café, 8 Lower O'Connell
Street, D1 (tel: 01-8780295);
Planet Web, 3 The Cobbles, Essex
Street, D2 (tel: 01-6772727).

Post
An Post is the state-operated national
post office. Postcard and letters
weighing less than 20 grammes cost
30p within Ireland and to all countries
within Europe. Letters and postcards to
countries outside Europe cost 45p. Most
post offices are open between 09.00 and
17.30 Monday to Friday, and on
Saturdays between 09.00 and 13.00. The
General Post Office (GPO) on O'Connell
Street is open between 08.00 and 20.00
Monday to Saturday, and on Sundays
and Holidays between 10.30 and 18.00.

Electricity
Standard voltage is 230 volts AC, or 50
hertz. Hotels will usually provide special
adaptors for any appliances you have
with you. If in doubt and you haven't left
for Ireland yet, ask your local electrical
dealer about a suitable transformer to
take with you.

Health
Visitors from EU countries are entitled to
medical treatment in Ireland and should
obtain a Form E111 from their National
Social Security office before they leave
home. These forms entitle the holder to
free treatment by a doctor whose name
appears on the Eastern Health Board list
(this list is available from Dr Steevens's
Hospital, Dublin 8, tel: 01-6790700). If
hospital treatment is necessary this will
be given free in a public ward. UK
visitors are entitled to all of the above
but do not require a Form E111. Visitors
from other countries should make sure
they have bought their medical cover at
home.
For a complete list of doctors and
dentists in the Dublin region, consult the
Golden Pages telephone directory,
available in all An Post offices and
Telecom Éireann offices.
A certain number of chemists/
pharmacies open till late. The following
stay open till 22.00 hours: **Leonard's
Corner Pharmacy,** 106 South Circular
Road, D2 (tel: 01-4534282);
O'Connell's, 55 O'Connell Street, D1
(tel: 01-8730427).

Emergencies
For emergency services such as Garda
Síochána (police), ambulance, fire
service, lifeboat and coastal rescue,
telephone 999 and ask for the service
you need. There is no charge for these
calls.

Petty Crime
Precautions you might take at home with
regard to petty crime should be kept in
mind when you are travelling around

Ireland, and especially when you are in Dublin. Tourists are a target for the bag snatcher, as they are in any city which attracts large numbers of tourists. Leave whatever valuables you can at your hotel or guesthouse and never leave any possessions on view in your car or camper van - the opportunist thief is rarely far away and seldom refuses an open invitation!

Cameras and Films

There are many camera shops throughout the city. They all provide a film development service. Most pharmacies sell film and many also provide a development service. The quickest and also the most expensive place to get your film developed is at the **One-Hour Photo** shops (there is one at the bottom of Grafton Street and another in the ILAC Shopping Centre off O'Connell Street). When you are buying your film, bear in mind that the weather, and therefore the light, can change very suddenly in Ireland.

Public Holidays

* 1 January - New Year's Day
* 17 March - St Patrick's Day
* Good Friday
* Easter Monday
* May Day
* 1st Monday in June - June Holiday
* 1st Monday in August - August Holiday
* Last Monday in October - October Holiday
* 25 December - Christmas Day
* 26 December - St Stephen's Day

Newspapers/Radio/TV

Dubliners consume news, opinion and gossip. The main Dublin-based Irish newspapers are **The Irish Times** and **Irish Independent**. The **Evening Herald** appears Monday to Saturday and is very useful for finding out what's on in the evening entertainment scene. The Irish Times appears Monday to Saturday and has a good 'What's On' column towards the back of the paper which lists a selection of museums, galleries, tours, recitals etc. that are open or on that day. The free fortnightly **Dublin Event Guide** (available in restaurants, cafés and pubs all over the city) and the fortnightly magazine **In Dublin** are both fairly comprehensive in their 'What's On' listings. You can buy most of the foreign newspapers in Dublin any day of the week. The best shops for foreign newspapers are **Eason's** on O'Connell Street, **Bus Stop** with outlets around the

city, and **Read's** on Nassau Street. The national broadcasting service, Radio Telefís Éireann (RTÉ), has three TV channels and three radio stations. Irish television is a mixture of Irish-produced news and current affairs programmes, a few Irish soaps, some good documentaries and a small amount of home-produced drama. The rest of the channel is taken up with foreign imports. By contrast, FM1, the principal RTÉ radio station, offers mainly home-produced programmes, much of it to a very high standard. 2FM is mainly a music station, while Radio na Gaeltachta broadcasts exclusively in the Irish language. In addition, there are numerous independent radio stations broadcasting in the Dublin region, most of them music stations with a few talk shows thrown in. Raidió na Life, a Dublin-based independent radio station broadcasting in the Irish language, was launched in 1993 and Telefís na Gaeilge (TnaG), a national TV channel in Irish, was launched in 1996.

Toilets

There are public toilets around the city, but many people prefer to avail of the toilets in pubs or the large department stores. Quite simply, in a city where petty crime is commonplace, few people will choose to descend the steps into one of the city's, albeit clean, public toilets when the option is there to use a secure indoor one.

Guides

Dublin Tourism on Suffolk Street (tel: 1850 230330) or Bord Fáilte, the Irish Tourist Board (tel: 01-6024000) will supply you with a list of all approved guides working in the Dublin region. They can be hired on a half-day or longer basis.

Genealogy

Many visitors to Ireland, in particular those from the USA, Canada and Australia, use some of their time in Dublin attempting to trace their family roots. It is best if some research is carried out before departure to Ireland and Bord Fáilte's Information Sheet No. 21 will help out in this respect. In Dublin, the **Genealogical Office**, 2 Kildare Street, D2 (tel: 01-6618811) is probably the best place to go to make enquiries. They will advise you on how to proceed with your research.

THINGS TO SEE AND DO

By international standards Dublin is not a large city and is really best discovered on foot. It is divided into a number of manageable touring days by the natural division of the River Liffey, and there is an increasing number of pedestrian streets in the inner city which makes walking the city less stressful than many cities of a similar size. There are three sections in Things To See And Do: *South of the Liffey*, *North of the Liffey* and *Best of the Rest*. All three sections are laid out to enable you see at a glance what one might call the *unmissable* places in Dublin. Thus, if you only have a day in Dublin, the Guide will help you be selective. Simply look for the places with a (✔) symbol. In any case, we have included everything of interest to the general visitor, whether you have the time to visit or not. All of the places in *South of the Liffey* and *North of the Liffey* can easily be reached on foot. The places in *Best of the Rest* are outside the inner city area and can be reached by public transport, by car, or if you are feeling energetic, by bicycle.

When out touring, be mindful of the fact that you are in a capital city. Not all Dubliners are angels and petty crime is no better or worse than most big cities. Tourists, being unfamiliar with the surroundings and being usually recognisable as tourists, can be the target of pick-pockets and muggers. Our advice is to leave all valuables secure in your accommodation, carry only the money you need for that day, and keep your wits about you. The chances of being picked out and robbed are very small, but you may avoid having to visit a local Garda (police) station with a sorry tale of stolen money or passport if you follow the above advice.

Now that you are ready to go out touring, enjoy the day! And remember, you can also follow any of the three Walking Tours described in *Three Classic Walks*.

South of the Liffey

1. Trinity College (✔) -   College Green

Founded by Queen Elizabeth I in 1592, Trinity College is the oldest university in Ireland. Nowadays it occupies a large piece of land in the centre of the city but when it was established it was due east of the medieval, walled city, occupying a site on which had stood the Augustinian Priory of All Hallows, founded by Dermot MacMurrough of Leinster.

Entering the College by the front gates you arrive in Parliament Square, also known as Front Square. You are immediately aware of a collegiate atmosphere. What is striking about Trinity is that this atmosphere exists despite the fact that the College, being open to the public, enjoys a constant flow of students, lecturers, and Joe and Mary Citizen alike. All merge freely and unproblematically in a university with 8,000 students. For the visitor the main attraction is the Library, a 64 m long building, whose oak ceiling was barrel-vaulted in an important addition to the building in 1859. The Library houses Ireland's most important collection of books, manuscripts and historical documents. The original building was built between 1712 and 1732 by Thomas Burgh. On the ground floor of the Library, in the Colonnades, can be seen the *Book of Kells*, an 8th-century illuminated manuscript containing the four Gospels, written in Latin and full of an exquisite array of complex and colourful illustrations.

It was found in the County Meath town of Kells, but was probably written by four individual monks on a monastery on the island of Iona, off the Scottish coast, sometime around AD 800. Also on display are the *Book of Armagh* and the *Book of Durrow*, both as old as the Book of Kells, and the medieval Irish harp, called *Brian Boru's Harp*.

Among the famous past students of Trinity were the writers Jonathan Swift, Oliver Goldsmith, Oscar Wilde, John Millington Synge and Samuel Beckett; the patriots Theobald Wolfe Tone, Robert Emmet, Henry Grattan and Thomas Davis; the philosophers George Berkeley and Edmund Burke. and more recently, the Irish President from 1990 to 1997, Mary Robinson.

Also See: **The Dublin Experience**, a 45-minute audio-visual exhibition tracing the history of Dublin from early times; Richard Castle's miniature **Printing House**, designed as a doric temple in 1734; William Chambers' **Chapel** (1798) and **Examination Hall** (1785) on Parliament Square, facing each other with matched porticos;

Deane and Woodward's magnificent **Museum Building** (1854), its dominant windows looking across College Park, its striking chimneys touching the skyline; Trinity's oldest building, the student residential **Rubrics** (1700) standing at the end of Library Square.

Opening Hours:
The Colonnades (all year) Mon-Sat 9.30-17.00 (last admission 17.00). Sun 12.00 (high season 09.30)-16.30 (last admission 16.30). Admission: Adults £4.50, Students/Senior Citizens £4, Family £9, Group rate £3.50.
Tel: (01) 6082308
The Dublin Experience may not operate in 1999 due to extensive construction work in the College grounds. Enquire at The Colonnades or at the College entrance.

Walking tours of the College take place every 15 minutes during the summer months from Front Square. The tour is lively and informative and the ticket includes entrance to The Colonnades/Book of Kells.

Trinity College.   Photo: Peter Zoeller.

2. Bank of Ireland - College Green

This 1729 building, across College Green from Trinity College, was originally the House of Parliament. Designed by Edward Lovett Pearce, additions east and west of the original portico involved the architects James Gandon and Robert Parke. After power was removed from the Irish Parliament by the Act of Union in 1800, the Bank of Ireland bought the building for £40,000 and they proceeded to convert the building for use as a bank. The extensive modifications were designed by Francis Johnston.

This is among the finest public buildings in Dublin. When the Bank of Ireland acquired it, the original House of Lords was kept as it had been during the heady years of Grattan's Parliament, when the Irish Parliament was operating in a semi-autonomous way from Westminster, between 1782 and 1800. **The House of Lords** is open to the public during banking hours. Two large tapestries (1733) which hang on

College Green with Trinity College and the Bank of Ireland. Photo: Peter Zoeller.

the walls depict two famous Protestant victories over Catholics: the Battle of the Boyne (1690) and the Siege of Derry (1689). Also in this chamber is a magnificent glass chandelier of

1788 and the House of Commons original Mace (1765). Guided tours of the Bank and its immediate environment are conducted every Tuesday by the Dublin writer and historian Éamonn MacThomáis. If you are in town on a Tuesday, it would be an hour or two well spent.
Opening Hours:
Mon-Fri 10.00–16.00 (Thurs till 17.00). *Tel: (01) 6776801.*

3. Temple Bar

Behind the Bank of Ireland is Temple Bar, a largely 18th-century district of the city. Stretching from Fishamble Street, to Westmoreland Street, and bounded by the River Liffey to the north and Dame Steet to the south, this compact and pedestrian-friendly part of the city began to take physical shape in the late 1600s. By the mid 1700s it was Dublin's busiest trading area. The original Custom House was situated where now stands the U2-owned Clarence Hotel. Many of the buildings which you can see today were designed and used as quayside warehouses. During the 1990s, the area underwent a radical transformation and is today the social heart of Dublin. Indeed, you will never go hungry or thirsty in Temple Bar, such is the number of restaurants and pubs on every street. There is also an interesting range of cultural activities in the area, most of which are open to the public. You can get all the information you need on the history and present-day activities of Temple Bar from the **Temple Bar Information Centre** on Eustace Street, open all year round.
Tel: (01) 6715717

4. Dublin Castle (✔)
Cork Hill

Built between 1204 and 1224, Dublin Castle was the seat of English power until it was handed over to the Irish provisional government in 1922, following the signing of the Anglo-Irish Treaty in the previous December. It was an imposing castle, ranking in form and construction with the great castles of Europe at the time. It was a roughly rectangular enclosure with four very substantial cylindrical towers at the corners, a twin-towered gateway in the centre of one long wall and a small turret near the centre of the opposite long wall. Most of the original structure has long since disappeared and today the main attractions for the visitor are the *State Apartments* and the *Undercroft*. The gloriously sumptuous State Apartments are a reminder of the kind of lifestyle the British-appointed Viceroys enjoyed during their sojourn in Dublin, while beneath street level the tour of the subterranean excavations are very interesting. The River Poddle converged with the Liffey at this point, forming a *Dubh Linn* (Gaelic for Black Pool), and it is generally accepted that the modern city's name originated here.

King John issued a writ authorising the construction of Dublin Castle in 1204 following advice that there was no place in which the royal treasure could safely be stored. In 1317 the Castle was threatened by Edward de Bruce, and in 1534 it was besieged, wholly unsuccessfully, by Silken Thomas Fitzgerald. Two famous escapes were made from the Castle, in 1591 and again in the following year, and both by the same man! Red Hugh O'Donnell, son of a Donegal chieftain, caused a minor sensation at the time by succeeding in lowering himself from a window in the Record Tower and escaping, twice!

Dublin Castle. Photo: Peter Zoeller.

Robert Emmet made a gallant but vain attempt at capturing the Castle in 1803, and on Easter Monday, 1916, Irish Volunteers and members of the Irish Citizen Army gained entry to the Castle grounds and held out for a day on the roof of City Hall before being captured.

Opening Hours: Mon-Fri 10.00-17.00. Sat/ Sun/Holidays 14.00-17.00. Admission: Adult £3, Child/Student/Senior Citizen £2. Children under 12 £1.
Tel: (01) 6777129.

5. City Hall -
Lord Edward Street

Unlike Paris, for example, Dublin is not a city of great perspectives. However the fine view from midway up Capel Street, looking south across Grattan Bridge to the splendid City Hall which returns the view, is a notable exception. The building was built as the Royal Exchange between 1769 and 1779, by Thomas Cooley. It is now the home of Dublin

Corporation. The classical facade and dome - impressive to view from inside the building - the urn-decorated balustrade, the fine marble statues of Daniel O'Connell and Henry Grattan and other important political figures, combine to make this one of Dublin's most important public buildings. The empty plinth between the main door and the balustrade was intended for the statue of Daniel O'Connell, but he is still indoors. City Hall looks down Parliament Street, the first street to be laid out by the Wide Streets Commissioners, in 1762. At that time the most easterly bridge across the Liffey was Essex (now Grattan) Bridge, thus all northside parliamentarians and others who had business to attend to in Parliament travelled this new street, probably by sedan chair or horse-drawn carriage. The buildings on the street and the street itself have been restored and given new life as part of the Temple Bar Renewal Project. The three statues in the small park beside City Hall were formerly part of the facade of the Royal University of Ireland on Earlsfort Terrace, a site now occupied by the National Concert Hall. They are said to represent three of the Dublin Guilds, none of which has survived.

Christ Church Cathedral.
Photo: Peter Zoeller.

6. Christ Church Cathedral
- Christchurch Place (✔)

On top of the hill of Dublin, Christ Church Cathedral (Cathedral of the Holy Trinity) commands the view. The Viking King Sigtryggr Silkbeard had a small, wooden church built here in 1038 for the first bishop of Dublin, Dunan. The Norman Earl of Pembroke, Richard de Clare (Strongbow) rebuilt the church in stone for the archbishop of Dublin, Laurence O'Toole, whose status was later raised to Saint Laurence, patron saint of Dublin. This church, which was begun in

1172, was still under construction in 1176 when Strongbow died, and also in 1180 when Laurence O'Toole died. A memorial to Strongbow can be seen in the present-day Cathedral's nave, while the heart of St Laurence is in a 13th-century reliquary in the chapel of St Laud, one of the Cathedral's small interior chapels. The crypt is the oldest intact building in Dublin, dating to the original construction in 1172. Over the centuries the Cathedral suffered many ignominies, not least the use being made of the vaults as taverns and the nave as a market in the late 1500s. In 1562 the nave vaulting collapsed bringing with it the south wall. The replacement was structurally unsound and the Cathedral was in such a state of disrepair by the mid 1800s that there was a real threat to its survival. Not to be outdone by Sir Benjamin Lee Guinness' magnanimous gesture in providing the money for the restoration of nearby St Patrick's Cathedral in 1864 (Guinness at the time was Dublin's largest employer and Sir Benjamin was carrying on a Guinness tradition of providing money for public projects in Dublin), Henry Roe, a Dublin whiskey distiller, stepped in with both the interest and the money required to save this great Cathedral. The architect George Edmund Street was commissioned to restore the building and the restoration took place between 1871 and 1878. Street's finished product was highly controversial, embellishing the main structure with elaborate flying buttresses and adding an annexe to the immediate west of the Cathedral. The restoration cost £250,000, quite a sum at that time.

All that remains above ground of the original Cathedral are the north wall, the transepts and the western part of the choir. In the grounds of the Cathedral are the chapter house remains of an Augustinian priory, abandoned at the time of the Reformation. The Cathedral is a fine example of early-Gothic architecture and the accompanying Romanesque sections which date to the late 12th century provide an interesting opportunity to view two clearly distinct styles of architecture.

Opening Hours: Daily 09.30-17.00 (till 17.30 during high season). Entrance charge is in the form of a donation request at the door. Adults £2, Children £1.
Tel: (01) 6778099

7. *Dublinia* - High Street

Across the road from Christ Church is St Michael's Church, built during the Christ Church restoration. Until recently the Synod Hall, it was bought by the Medieval Trust whose new, state-of-the-art exhibition covers the

period of Dublin life from the arrival of the Anglo-Normans in 1170 to the closure of its monasteries in 1540. Included in the exhibition are life-like displays of memorable episodes in the history of that period; a scale model of the medieval city; life-size reconstructions based on the 13th-century dockside at Wood Quay and a 15th-century merchant's house; a collection of genuine artifacts from the National Museum of Ireland; and an audio-visual presentation in the Great Hall.

Opening Hours: Apr-Sept: Daily 10.00-17.00. Oct-Mar: Mon-Sat 11.00-16.00. Sun. 10.00-16.30. Admission (includes visit to Christ Church Cathedral): Adults £3.95, Student/Senior Citizen £2.90, Family £10, Group rate £3.50, Under 5's free.
Tel: (01) 6794611

St Patrick's Cathedral and Marsh's Library.   Photo: Peter Zoeller.

8. *St Patrick's Cathedral* - Patrick Street (✔)

Several hundred metres south of Christ Church stands Dublin's second great Protestant cathedral. St Patrick's was founded on possibly the earliest Christian site in Dublin, a place where St Patrick is said to have baptised local people in the 5th century. A small, wooden church probably existed at the site as early as AD 450. Confusion exists as to the actual year of the foundation of the present Cathedral, but it is commonly held to be 1191. It acquired Cathedral status in 1213, and the famous Minot Tower was added in 1362. Like its near neighbour, St Patrick's had a turbulent history and by 1864 the building was, by all accounts, on its last legs. Sir Benjamin Lee Guinness came to the rescue, donating £160,000 towards its restoration and overseeing the four-year work by the architect Sir Thomas Drew. Like Christ Church, the restoration was severely criticised at the time by people who felt the original structure was not well reflected in the restoration. For a time, in fact, the Cathedral was irreverently referred to as the *Brewer's Church*, after Sir Benjamin himself. Between 1901 and 1904, a successor to Benjamin Lee Guinness, Lord Iveagh, undertook a full restoration of the choir. It was at this time that the adjoining St Patrick's Park was excavated and laid out as public gardens. During the excavation work remains of St Patrick's Well were discovered just north of the tower. Jonathan Swift was Dean of St Patrick's from 1713 until his death in 1745. He is buried near where you enter the Cathedral, and lies beside his lifelong companion, Stella Johnston. The Cathedral is almost overflowing with monuments and it can be a little bewildering if you try to absorb each one. Among the most important are mementoes to Swift, some Celtic gravestones, medieval brasses and tiles, memorials to the blind harper and composer, Carolan, the composer William Balfe, and the first President of Ireland, Douglas Hyde. An interesting item is the Door of Reconciliation which faces you as you enter the Cathedral. The fascinating story attached to this relic can be read

on the small plaque nearby.
Opening Hours: Open all year round. Mon-Fri 09.00-18.00. Sat 09.00-17.00. Sun Apr-Sept 09.30-17.00. Sun Oct-Mar 10.00-15.00. Restricted viewing on Sun during Services. Admission: Adults £2, Students/Senior Citizens £1.50, Family £5, Group rate £1.75.
Tel: (01) 4754817

9. Marsh's Library
- St Patrick's Close

Beside St Patrick's Cathedral is Marsh's Library, the oldest public library in Ireland, founded in 1701 by Archbishop Narcissus Marsh and opened in 1707. The building was designed by Sir William Robinson who had earlier designed the Royal Hospital Kilmainham (*see Best of the Rest*). The interior of the Library is unchanged since the 18th century. An interesting feature are the three wired alcoves within which readers consulted rare books that were chained to the walls. The Library contains some 25,000 books, some dating from the 16th century, together with 250 volumes of manuscripts and many maps.
Opening Hours: All year round. Mon-Fri 10.00-12.45 and 14.00-17.00. **Tues closed**. Sat 10.30-12.45. Admission: A donation is requested, Adults £1.
Tel: (01) 4543511

10. St Werburgh's Church
- Werburgh Street

Directly across Christchurch Place from Christ Church Cathedral and around the corner on which stands the Lord Edward Pub, is nestled modestly the lovely church of St Werburgh. A fire destroyed much of the interior of Thomas Burgh's original 1715 church and the church you see today was rebuilt in 1759. Because of anxieties among the Dublin Castle authorities about the possibility of the tower and spire of St Werburgh's being used by rebels against the Castle (the spire overlooked the Castle courtyard) the authorities declared it unsafe in 1810 and demolished it. The body of Lord Edward Fitzgerald who was killed during the rebellion of 1798 is interred in the church's vault. The church has one the finest 18th-century church interiors in Dublin, however it is not open to the public. A stone's throw from here, in Hoey's Court in 1667, Jonathan Swift was born. A social welfare office marks the spot today.

11. St Audoen's Churches - High Street

West of Christ Church Cathedral on the same side of the street is the Catholic St Audoen's Church, built in 1846 with the fine Corinthian columns being added in 1899. Just past this church is the much older and more interesting Protestant church of St Audoen. Built on an early Christian site of St Columcille's church, the building you see today dates partly from the 12th century (the tower and main door) and the 15th century (the aisle) and the 19th-century restoration. Ireland's three oldest bells ring out from the tower, the oldest dating from 1423. Some historians claim that some of the remains of the early St Columcille's church were incorporated into the 12th-century building. If you turn right when you leave the church and go down the stone path you will be walking down towards the only surviving gate of the old walled city of Dublin. This is St Audoen's Arch and it

dates to 1240. The street outside the old gate is Cook Street (*see A Walking Tour of Medieval Dublin*) and at the western end of this street, on Bridge Street, is the oldest pub in Dublin, the Brazen Head.

12. The Liberties

Many visitors to Dublin hear about the famous Liberties yet can seldom identify where they are. Indeed, many Dubliners would be unable to tell you why they are called Liberties. They roughly incorporate the area to the immediate south and west of Christ Church Cathedral, and more precisely are bounded by Fishamble Street, southwards along Werburgh and Bride Streets, westwards along Long Lane to Malpas Street and Blackpitt, and northwards from there up through Pimlico and Bridgefoot Street. Within its approximate boundaries are many interesting buildings. In addition

Photo: Peter Zoeller.

to the two cathedrals of Christ Church and St Patrick's, St Werburgh's and St Audoen's Churches and Marsh's Library, there are the Iveagh Markets in Francis Street, the Augustinian Church in Thomas Street with its marvellous spire dominating the area around Thomas Street, and several other interesting churches. In medieval Dublin, there were a number of districts outside the city walls which did not come under the jurisdiction of the civic authorities. Each individual district had its own manor court. In the 17th century Protestant Huguenots, under persecution in France, fled to Dublin and established a thriving weaving industry. Such was the success of their endeavours that Dutch and Flemish weavers came to the Liberties to set up businesses, and some Dutch Billy houses survived up to the 1960s. During the 19th century much of the Liberties became slums which housed the despairing poor of Dublin. In more recent times new Dublin Corporation housing schemes have helped to revitalise the area, while even more recently private developers have capitalised on generous tax incentives to create a string of new, private apartment blocks. Regrettably, these private developments leave much to be desired on the aesthetic level, representing as they do a boring and bland architecture, like much else of Dublin's more recent developments.

13. St Catherine's Church
- Thomas Street

Walking from Christ Church Cathedral towards Guinness Brewery, St Catherine's Church is on your left, on Thomas Street. Completed in 1769, it was built on the site of a 12th-century church whose original construction was to honour Thomas à Becket, Archbishop of Canterbury, on the orders of King Henry II. In 1803 the patriot Robert Emmet was hanged across the street from the church. The building was restored recently by the Church of Ireland organisation, CORE, as a place of worship for all denominations.

14. Guinness Brewery and Hop Store (✔)
- St James's Gate

Destined to go down in Dublin folklore though not knowing it at the time, Arthur Guinness bought Rainsford Brewery in 1759 and established his brewing firm up at St James's Gate, a short walk west from Christ Church Cathedral. Although the brewery did not initially produce stout (it was then known as porter, originating from the porters in London's Covent Garden whose

Guinness Brewery.   Photo: Peter Zoeller.

favoured drink it was), when it commenced brewing the Guinness stout we all know today, the brewery quickly became the largest in Dublin; at one stage it was the largest in the world, with over 4,000 employees. There was no shortage of competition - no fewer than 55 breweries were producing beer of varying quality in Dublin in 1800 - but nor was there a shortage of consumers, for it was said that the vice of drinking was one of the greatest evils during this period and that ale-houses formed one-third of the total number of houses in Dublin. An extension to the Grand Canal brought the waterway into the Guinness complex in order that the porter could be transported by horse-drawn barge to Limerick, Ballinasloe in County Galway, and eastwards to Ringsend where it was exported by ship. The brewery extended down to the Liffey and in 1872 it was operating ten barges to and from a point just downriver from Heuston Bridge.

The oldest part of the brewery is behind some offices on the south side of James's Street. In medieval times St James's Gate was one of the fortified gates leading into the old walled city. The brewery today occupies some 60 acres, but it also has offices all over the world, being now a multi-owned, multi-national corporation. Nonetheless, it is still regarded as an entirely Dublin institution, an institution which produces over 10 million glasses of the creamy-topped porter every day!

The philanthropic deeds of some of the Guinness proprietors over the years have greatly enhanced the city. Sir Benjamin Lee Guinness, grandson of Arthur, restored St Patrick's Cathedral; Benjamin's son, Lord Ardilaun, rebuilt the Coombe Maternity Hospital in 1877, and laid out St Stephen's Green for the public in 1880; his brother, Lord Iveagh, helped to finance a new wing of the Rotunda Hospital and also laid out St Patrick's Park, the attractive park beside the Cathedral, for the public in 1903.

The Guinness Hop Store on Crane Street, off James's Street, is in a converted 19th-century warehouse. Visitors can watch an audio-visual show on the history of Guinness and visit the museum. There is also, of course, a bar at which you are encouraged to 'sample the goods'. There used to be a belief, fairly

commonplace, that Guinness does not travel well. If this is true the Hop Store Guinness must be a mighty fine brew indeed!
Hop Store Opening Hours:
Open all year round. Mon-Fri 10.00-16.30. Closed Holidays. Last programme starts at 15.30. Admission: Adults £3, Children £1, Groups of 20 plus £2. *Tel: (01) 4538364.*

15. Kilmainham Gaol

Kilmainham Gaol ceased to function as a jail in 1924, two years after it incarcerated prisoners from the losing side in the Civil War, including Éamon de Valera who would later become Taoiseach (Prime Minister) and later again President of Ireland in 1959. Six years before de Valera spent time in the jail, leaders of the failed Easter Rising of 1916 had been impounded in the gloomy prison cells. Fourteen of these, including Patrick Pearse and his young brother Willie, and the crippled James Connolly who had been wounded in the leg during the fighting, were executed in the jail's yard in the days following the Rising. Prior to that, leaders of rebellions in 1798, 1803, 1848 and 1867 were detained in the jail. Among its most illustrious 'guests' were Robert Emmet and Charles Stewart Parnell. The jail was opened as a museum by Éamon de Valera in 1966. There is a guided tour, an audio-visual presentation and an exhibition. A multi-media exhibition showing material from the Gaol's archives opened at the end of April 1996.
Opening Hours: Apr-Sept: daily 09.30-16.45 (last admission). Oct-Mar: Mon-Fri 09.30-16.00 (last admission), Sun 10.00-16.45 (last admission). Closed Sat. Admission: Adults £3, Child/Student £1.25, Senior Citizen £2, Family £7.50. Group rate available. *Tel: (01) 4535984.* Last admission 1 hour before closing.

16. Royal Hospital Kilmainham / Irish Museum of Modern Art (IMMA)

Opening Hours: Open all year. Tues-Sat 10.00-17.30. Sun 12.00-17.30. Closed Mon.
Admission: Free.
Tel: (01) 6129900

The architectural style of the Royal Hospital in Kilmainham, close to Kilmainham Gaol, is based on Les Invalides in Paris. With a formal facade, spacious courtyard and fine interior, it is arguably Ireland's finest 17th-century monumental building. It was designed by Sir William Robinson and completed in 1685 and served as a home for retired soldiers for almost 250 years, at the same time that the Chelsea Hospital in London was offering similar services. The Royal Hospital clients were frequently referred to as _Chelsea pensioners._ In 1986 the Irish Government restored the long since defunct building at a cost of £21 million and in 1991 it reopened its doors as the Irish Museum of Modern Art (IMMA). The Museum

17. Whitefriars Carmelite Church - Aungier Street

There was an ancient belief that birds mated on 14 February. As a result, girls would choose their partner on that day. St Valentine's feastday fell on this date, and thus did the saint become synonymous with the romantic aspect of St Valentine's Day which in modern times has grown into a commercial phenomenon. The remains of St Valentine are contained in this church, which was built in 1827 and considerably altered in 1856 and 1868. The church stands on the former site of a pre-Reformation Carmelite Priory, founded in 1278 and suppressed by Henry VIII in 1537. The present church has a number of interesting items on display, among them the 16th-century Flemish oak statue of the Virgin and Child. This is possibly the only survivor of its kind from the wholesale theft and destruction of churches which took place during the Reformation.

Royal Hospital Kilmainham.
Photo: Peter Zoeller.

houses a permanent collection of Irish and international art of the 20th century, as well as visiting exhibitions throughout the year. In addition, the annual programme features live music and theatrical performances.

18. St Andrew's Church - St Andrew Street

If you look across the street from the front steps of the Bank of Ireland you will see the spire of St Andrew's Church rising behind the Ulster Bank on College Green. This Protestant church (1860-73) was built on the site of the nunnery of St Mary de Hogge. While the building itself is not especially notable, its location is, for it was on a higher mound of earth across the street from the church that the old Viking parliament carried out its business of enacting laws, passing sentences etc. The parliament was called the 'Thingmote' and the 40 foot high ceremonial mound was excavated in 1661 to fill in the marshy laneway which today runs along the side of Trinity College as Nassau Street. The building was recently renovated and is now the main city-centre tourist office.

19. Grafton Street (✔)

The pedestrian Grafton Street, which leads from College Green to St Stephen's Green, is regarded by many today as the centre of Dublin, although geographically O'Connell Bridge would be closer to the mark. Before being pedestrianised in 1982, it was an important traffic artery and was always a busy street. Several recent facelifts, including the upgrading of the street furniture and the laying of a redbrick street paving to replace the old tarmac road, have transformed it into a highly successful retail thoroughfare. Here rents soar and traditional businesses are finding that life in the fast lane of 1990s high-street selling is not so easy. Still, many of the old shops have survived, not least Weir's Jewellers with its beautiful traditional front. Beside Bewley's Oriental Café, at No. 79, was once Whyte's Academy whose pupils included Richard Brinsley Sheridan, Thomas Moore, Robert Emmet and Arthur Wellesley, later to become the Duke of Wellington. In recent years, Grafton Street has attracted the most talented buskers in the city. When evening falls, the streets off Grafton Street are crowded with diners and revellers in the many restaurants and pubs in the area.

20. Powerscourt Townhouse - South William Street

During the second half of the 18th-century many elegant and exquisitely decorated townhouses were designed by leading architects of the day for wealthy and often powerful residents. One of these was the Powerscourt family whose principal residence was in County Wicklow. Lord Powerscourt engaged the services of Robert Mack - he had earlier designed Essex (now Grattan) Bridge - to design a townhouse dwelling. A fine site was chosen, between Parliament House on College Green and the fashionable St Stephen's Green, and in 1774 the impressive townhouse was completed. By the time the building was sold to a textile firm in 1835, the land surrounding the house had been developed and the

Grafton Street.   Photo: Peter Zoeller.

---

the nunnery of St Mary de Hogge. While the building itself is not especially notable, its location is, for it was on a higher mound of earth across the street from the church that the old Viking parliament carried out its business of enacting laws, passing sentences etc. The parliament was called the 'Thingmote' and the 40 foot high ceremonial mound was excavated in 1661 to fill in the marshy laneway which today runs along the side of Trinity College as Nassau Street. The building was recently renovated and is now the main city-centre tourist office.

19. Grafton Street (✔)

The pedestrian Grafton Street, which leads from College Green to St Stephen's Green, is regarded by many today as the centre of Dublin, although geographically O'Connell Bridge would be closer to the mark. Before being pedestrianised in 1982, it was an important traffic artery and was always a busy street. Several recent facelifts, including the upgrading of the street furniture and the laying of a redbrick street paving to replace the old tarmac road, have transformed it into a highly successful retail thoroughfare. Here rents soar and traditional businesses are finding that life in the fast lane of 1990s high-street selling is not so easy. Still, many of the old shops have survived, not least Weir's Jewellers with its beautiful traditional front. Beside Bewley's Oriental Café, at No. 79, was once Whyte's Academy whose pupils included Richard Brinsley Sheridan, Thomas Moore, Robert Emmet and Arthur Wellesley, later to become the Duke of Wellington. In recent years, Grafton Street has attracted the most talented buskers in the city. When evening falls, the streets off Grafton Street are crowded with diners and revellers in the many restaurants and pubs in the area.

20. Powerscourt Townhouse - South William Street

During the second half of the 18th-century many elegant and exquisitely decorated townhouses were designed by leading architects of the day for wealthy and often powerful residents. One of these was the Powerscourt family whose principal residence was in County Wicklow. Lord Powerscourt engaged the services of Robert Mack - he had earlier designed Essex (now Grattan) Bridge - to design a townhouse dwelling. A fine site was chosen, between Parliament House on College Green and the fashionable St Stephen's Green, and in 1774 the impressive townhouse was completed. By the time the building was sold to a textile firm in 1835, the land surrounding the house had been developed and the

Grafton Street.   Photo: Peter Zoeller.

building became indistinct among the newer developments. In the 1980s the house and courtyard were cleverly converted into a glass-roofed shopping centre, with an interesting array of small shops, restaurants and craft stalls. A 1998 upgrade improved the Centre even further. Today the Powerscourt Townhouse Shopping Centre is easily the most attractive of the Dublin shopping complexes. It links Grafton Street with South Great George's Street, forming one of the city's more interesting pedestrian areas.

21. Dublin Civic Museum - South William Street

The intimate Dublin Civic Museum is a few steps from the South William Street entrance to the Powerscourt Townhouse. It houses an unusual exhibition of artifacts collected, donated, bought and found, all pertaining to the history of Dublin in all its glory but also in its minutest detail. It is a collection which generates much nostalgia for Dubliners, but like most museums, foreign visitors are more common than the native species. A particularly interesting exhibit is the damaged, carved head of Admiral Nelson, who once cast his gaze over all the city from the top of O'Connell Street's Nelson Pillar, until the IRA unceremoniously brought him and his towering Doric column to the ground when they blew up the monument in 1966.
Opening Hours: Open all year Tues-Sat 10.00-18.00. Sun 11.00-14.00. Closed Mon.
Admission: Free.
Tel: (01) 6794260

22. St Stephen's Green (✔)

Dublin is lucky to have some beautiful parks, none more so than St Stephen's Green. It was formally laid out and opened to the public in 1880 by Arthur Edward Guinness, then proprietor of the Guinness Brewery and later to become Lord Ardilaun. Prior to that the Green was enclosed since 1663, when for a time the west side was a place of execution and a nearby leper colony. During the latter half of the 18th century the north side was known as the _Beaux' Walk_, where the aristocracy strolled in their elegant attire. The north side remains to this day the most fashionable, overlooked as it is by the exclusive and very graceful Victorian Shelbourne Hotel whose bars are the social home to many a Dublin jet-setter.
If you have the time, a nice way to explore the Green is to begin by walking the four sides, outside the railings. Starting at the top of Grafton Street and walking south towards Harcourt Street you will pass a statue of Robert Emmet, who died a patriot at the age of 23 in 1803. He faces his demolished birthplace at No. 124. Just beyond Emmet is the seated statue of Lord Ardilaun with his head inclined towards St James Gate, home of the Guinness Brewery, of which he was the proprietor at the time. Directly opposite him is the Royal College of Surgeons, famous medical college and one of the locations of the 1916 Easter Rising.
Continuing around to the south side of the Green you will come across the seat commemorating 'James Joyce, Dubliner, John Stanislaus Joyce, Corkonian' (James's father). The seat faces Newman House, where Joyce studied from 1899 to 1902 (see 24), and University Church, a popular church among post-graduates of University College Dublin (UCD) for marriage

ceremonies. On the same side, further east, is Iveagh House, now the home of the Department of Foreign Affairs and one time home of Sir Benjamin Lee Guinness, restorer of St Patrick's Cathedral. The east side of the Green conveys the best impression of a Georgian streetscape of all the four sides - though some of the houses are reconstructions - while the north side possesses some imposing buildings, among them the Shelbourne Hotel, the Friendly Brothers' House at No. 22, the University Club (1776-8) at No. 17, the St Stephen's Green Club (1756) at No. 9, where Sir Walter Scott stayed in 1825, and the United Services Club (1754) at No. 8.

Entering the Green from the top of Grafton Street you pass through the Fusiliers' Arch, commemorating the 212 Irish soldiers who died in the Boer War of 1899-1902. In the park itself there are some interesting monuments and memorials, notably that of Henry Moore's unusual sculpture of William Butler Yeats (1967). Near the pond - which is home to many species of duck and geese - is the central section of the park and where you can sit on one of the many seats and admire the scene. There are some interesting busts nearby, in particular that of James Clarence Mangan, a Dublin poet who died in poverty (1803-49),

St Stephen's Green.   Photo: Peter Zoeller.

and Countess Markievicz, one of the 1916 Rising insurrectionists. In 1918, she became the first woman to be elected to the British House of Commons, although she refused to take her seat. Directly south of the central area and just before you leave the Green, is a bronze bust of James Joyce, exactly opposite Newman House. The south-east corner of the Green has an interesting bronze sculpture of three female figures over a fountain, presented to the Irish Government in 1956 by West Germany in recognition of Irish aid after the Second World War. Two sculptures at the north-east side, near the Shelbourne Hotel, are worth seeing. Outside the railings is Edward Delaney's bronze statue of Theobald Wolfe Tone, leader of the United Irishmen and insurrection of 1798, and of the failed French expedition to Ireland that same year. Behind this statue, just inside the Green, is a memorial to those who died from starvation in the 1845-8 Famine.

23. The Royal College of Surgeons ↝ St Stephen's Green

The prominent building on the west side of St Stephen's Green is the Royal College of Surgeons, built to the design of William Murray between 1825 and 1827, with a much later addition behind the original building, on York Street. The building was occupied by a brigade of the Irish Volunteers during the 1916 Easter Rising and damage from British army firepower can be seen on the front stonework. One of the Volunteers, Countess Markievicz, featured prominently in the skirmishes. She was born Constance Gore-Booth, educated in Sligo and entered into the Anglo-Irish landed gentry class. In 1908 she became committed to the nationalist cause and joined Sinn Féin. After the Easter Rising she was sentenced to death but was released in the general amnesty of 1917. In 1918 she was the first woman to be elected to the British House of Commons, however in keeping with Sinn Féin's policy she refused to take up her seat. During the *Troubles*, the common term which described the years of struggle before Independence, she was constantly on the run and served

Newman House. Photo: Newman House.

two jail sentences. She was a stringent opponent of the Anglo-Irish Treaty of 1921 and in 1926 she joined the Fianna Fáil Party founded by Éamon de Valera. She was re-elected to the Dáil (Irish Parliament) the following year but, in failing health, she died later that year. A remarkable

woman, she is buried in Glasnevin cemetery.

24. Newman House
- St Stephen's Green

On the south side of the Green, at Nos. 85/86, stands Newman House. No. 85 was designed by Richard Castle in 1739 for a Member of Parliament, Hugh Montgomery. No. 86 was built for Richard 'Burn Chapel' Whaley in 1765 by Robert West. Whaley was a Member of Parliament and a noted priest hater. His infamous son and rake, 'Buck' Whaley, became an MP when he was still a teenager and was a lifelong gambler. The well known stuccodores, the Francini brothers from Switzerland, were engaged and their superb plasterwork, particularly in the Apollo Room, stand out as among the very finest in the entire city.

Both houses were acquired in 1865 by the Catholic University of Ireland. The 19-century writer and theologian John Henry Newman was its first rector and the houses were named after him. James Joyce attended college here between 1899 and 1902. Gerard Manley Hopkins was Professor of Classics between 1884 until his death in 1899. He lived upstairs in No. 86 and his study has been restored and opened for public viewing. Others who studied here were the Dublin writer Flann O'Brien and two leading figures in the 1916 Easter Rising, Patrick Pearse and Éamon de Valera.

Opening Hours: June-Aug: Tues-Fri 12.00-17.00. Sat 14.00-17.00. Sun 11.00-14.00. Closed Mon. Admission: Adults £2, Students/Senior Citizens/Children £1. Group rate 30p.
Tel: (01) 7067422. Open for group tours by appointment all year.

25. Iveagh House
St Stephen's Green

Iveagh House today houses the Department of Foreign Affairs. It was donated to the State by Rupert Guinness, second Earl of Iveagh, in 1939. Previously it had been owned by Sir Benjamin Lee Guinness who had acquired the house in 1866. He transformed Richard Castle's original 1730s building, changing the facade and adding a richly decorated ballroom. It was the German-born architect's first Dublin design but nothing of his original facade remains.

26. Fitzwilliam Square

If you leave the Green at the south-east corner and walk up Lower Leeson Street, turning left into Pembroke Street, you will come across the smallest, and the last to be completed, of the five Georgian squares in the city. This is Fitzwilliam Square, built over a period of thirty-five years, between 1791 and 1825. Its completion signalled the end of a unique period of building which lasted almost one hundred years. It is the only Georgian square whose park is still reserved for residents. The houses around it are smaller than in the other four squares (Merrion, St Stephen's, Parnell and Mountjoy) but they are extremely well preserved. The doorways, which are regularly painted in bright colours, are a particularly attractive feature. Traditionally, members of the legal profession were associated with the Square, but nowadays the medical profession are more in evidence.

27. 29 Lower Fitzwilliam Street

This fine Georgian house, built in 1794 for a Mrs Olivia Beatty, was recently restored, decorated and furnished in the style of a typical Georgian townhouse of the period. It is extremely well executed and for anyone interested in how the nobility and gentry lived at the end of the 18th century in Dublin, this is undoubtedly the place to go. The principal promoters of the restoration project were the Electricity Supply Board (ESB) who probably felt obliged to restore part of Dublin's heritage, as well as their public image, after their widely condemned decision to demolish about 20 fine Georgian houses on Fitzwilliam Street Lower in 1961, to make way for their new, modern and very bland headquarters. The National Museum were also involved in the restoration.
Opening Hours: Open all year. Tues-Sat 10.00-17.00. Sun 14.00-17.00. Closed Mon.
Admission: Adults £2.50, Children to age 16 free, Students/ Unwaged/Senior Citizens £1.
Tel: (01) 7026165

28. Merrion Square (✔)

Built for the nobility and the gentry, like all the Georgian squares, Merrion Square is today considered the heart of Georgian Dublin. It was laid out by architect John Ensor in the 1760s, the north and east sides being the first to be completed. The west side is dominated by the lawn of Leinster House (Dáil Éireann), the National Gallery and the Natural History Museum. The houses on the Square are fine examples of 18th-century townhouses, with their uniform height and use of materials, the fine doorways with distinct brass door knockers and letter boxes, the often ornate, half-moon, glass sunlights over the doors, the wrought ironwork along some of the balconies and the long windows of the first-floor drawing-rooms where guests were entertained at lavish parties during each parliamentary term. The east side of the Square continues in a pleasing vista of 18th-century townhouses all the way up Fitzwilliam Street from Holles Street Maternity Hospital at the north-east corner. This was once the longest line of uninterrupted Georgian townhouses anywhere in Europe, a record broken by unfortunate development along the east side of Fitzwilliam Street in 1961.

Many famous names are associated with Merrion Square, among them Sir William Wilde and his wife, 'Speranza' who lived in No. 1 with their son,

Merrion Square. Photo: Peter Zoeller.

Oscar; Daniel O'Connell the great 'Liberator' and driving force behind the campaign for Catholic Emancipation - partly achieved in 1829 - who lived in No. 58; the poet, William Butler Yeats, who lived for a time in No. 52, and later in No. 82.

29. National Gallery (✔) - Merrion Square

The National Gallery opened to the public in 1864, ten years after

it was established by an Act of Parliament. One year earlier, the railway magnate William Dargan, whose statue stands on the lawn in front of the Gallery, had organised a huge industrial exhibition on the adjoining Leinster Lawn: the paintings which were shown as part of that exhibition formed the nucleus of the Gallery's early collection. Nowadays the Gallery has an impressive collection of paintings representing the major European schools, as well as an appropriately strong collection of Irish painting. A statue of George Bernard Shaw stands inside the Dargan Wing on the ground floor. Shaw left one-third of his estate to the National Gallery in recognition of the contribution his regular visits here made to his education.

Among the highlights of a visit to the Gallery are a viewing of the magnificent *Taking of Christ* by Caravaggio, recently discovered hanging in a Dublin Jesuit college and restored with great care by the Gallery's chief restorer, Sergio Benedetti; the Dargan Wing's ground floor with its impressive display of full-length portraits and the beautiful Waterford crystal chandeliers hanging from the ceiling; the fine collection of Irish paintings on the ground floor of the Milltown Wing, particularly the room devoted to the work of Jack Yeats, brother of William Butler Yeats. The Gallery has undergone extensive renovations over recent years and further developments are planned.

<u>*Opening Hours:*</u> Open all year round. Mon-Sat 10.00-17.15, Thurs till 20.15. Sun 14.00-17.00. Admission: Free. There are guided tours on Sat at 14.15, 15.00 and on Sun at 15.00 and 16.00. *Tel: (01) 6615133.*

The Gallery possesses an excellent bookshop and a very popular restaurant.

30. Natural History Museum - Merrion Square

Immediately south of Leinster Lawn is the Natural History Museum, housing a large collection of stuffed animals from all over the world, with a comprehensive collection of Irish mammals.
Opening Hours: Open all year round. Tues-Sat 10.00-17.00. Sun 14.00-17.00. Closed Mon. Admission: Free.
Tel: (01) 6777444

31. Government Buildings - Upper Merrion Street

Immediately south of the Natural History Museum are the imposing Government Buildings, with forbidding iron gates and domed building behind the entrance. These were built in 1911 for the Royal College of Science but are now entirely given over to Government use. Some years ago, under the former Taoiseach (Prime Minister) Charles J. Haughey, a reputed £20 million was spent on restoring these buildings. They have since become known as the 'Chas Mahal'!
Opening Hours: There are guided tours of Government Buildings on Saturday. Tickets available from the National Gallery ticket office. Admission: Free. For information on tour times, _Tel: (01) 6624888._

Directly opposite Government Buildings is No. 24 Merrion Street Upper. Recently subsumed into a five-star hotel, the house was formerly known as Mornington House and is believed to be the birthplace of Arthur Wellesley, Duke of Wellington, although the town of Trim in County Meath also lays claim to this fact (see _Boyne Valley Tour_ in _Excursions Outside Dublin_).

32. Leinster House - Kildare Street

Leinster House (1745-8) was designed by the German-born architect, Richard Castle, who established himself as one of Ireland's most influential architects of the Georgian period. He was commissioned by the Earl of Kildare to design a significant town mansion on a vacant site south-east of Trinity College. The Earl, who in 1766 became Duke of Leinster, reputedly never liked the house, it being far too large and anonymous for his needs. The back of the house faces onto Leinster Lawn (_view from Merrion Square_) and the obelisk in the centre of this lawn commemorates the founders of

Leinster House.   Photo: Peter Zoeller.

the Irish State, Arthur Griffiths, Michael Collins and Kevin O'Higgins.

In 1815 the Dublin Society (later the Royal Dublin Society) bought the house and in 1922 the Parliament of the newly-established Irish Free State moved in. Today, 166 Members of Parliament (TDs) sit in the Dáil (Lower House), while a further 60 senators carry on their business in the Seanad (Senate). It is possible to gain access to the public gallery but you usually have to be invited by a TD. Enquire at the gate.

33. National Museum (✔)
- Kildare Street

A visit to the National Museum on Kildare Street is an obligatory visit, such is the importance of its collection of historical artifacts. The building was built in 1890 to a design by Thomas Newenham Deane and faces across the courtyard of Dáil Éireann to the National Library. The Museum is easy to walk around, well laid out, and some of the exhibitions are breathtaking. Among the highlights are the Irish Gold exhibition which features the finest collection of prehistoric gold artifacts in Europe; the Treasury exhibition which includes such remarkable works of Early Christian Art as the Ardagh Chalice, the Tara Brooch and the Cross of Cong; Viking Age Ireland which focuses on Irish archaeology from 800 to 1200 AD; and the Road to Independence exhibition which deals with Irish history from 1900 to the 1921 Anglo-Irish Treaty, with particularly interesting items from the 1916 Easter Rising. Collins Barracks opened in 1997 as Ireland's new national museum of decorative arts and its economic, social, political and military history. On display are artifacts ranging from weaponry, furniture, folklife and costume to silver, ceramics and glassware. Located in a converted army barracks.

Opening Hours: Open all year round. Tues-Sat 10.00-17.00. Sun 14.00-17.00. Closed Mon. Admission: Free. Guided tours of the Museum: £1.
Tel: (01) 6777444.
Buses: 90 (Aston Quay), 25, 25A, 66, 67 (Middle Abbey Street). Both museums have a shop and a café.

Treasures at the National Museum.
Photo: National Museum.

34. National Library
- Kildare Street

Facing across the courtyard of Leinster House is a similar-looking building to the National Museum. This is the National Library (1884-90) and it was designed and built at the same

time as the National Museum, by Thomas Newenham Deane and his son. Original occupiers of all three adjoining buildings was the Royal Dublin Society, then the Dublin Society. Today the National Library is a rich source of archive material, with newspapers and books of historic and social interest available for consultation purposes. Visitors may apply for a reading ticket, but may be referred to the ILAC Centre Library near O'Connell Street. The Reading Room of the National Library is featured in James Joyce's *Ulysses*.
Opening Hours: Open all year. Mon-Wed 10.00-21.00. Thurs-Fri 10.00-16.45. Sat 10.00-12.45. Closed Sun. Admission: Free.
Tel: (01) 6618811

35. Heraldic Museum & Genealogical Office
- Kildare St/Nassau St

On the corner of Kildare Street and Nassau Street is the fine, Venetian-style, red-brick building which was once the home of the conservative Kildare Street Club. Built in 1860-61 by Thomas Deane and Benjamin Woodward, its interior was irretrievably altered for the worse when the northern half of the building was bought in 1971 by the Phoenix Assurance Company. Today, the building contains the Heraldic Museum and the Genealogical Office. It is in the latter that you would make initial enquiries about your Irish roots. The building also contains the Alliance Française which offers among other cultural activities regular classes in the French language.

36. Mansion House
- Dawson Street

The Mansion House is the residence and office of the Lord Mayor of Dublin. Most Lord Mayors jump at the opportunity to live in this sumptuous Queen Anne-style 1710 building for the one-year period of the mayoralty. The Lord Mayor of Dublin is elected by Dublin City Council every year and his or her role is a very high profile one, though not particularly powerful. The house was built for Sir Joshua Dawson but he ran into financial difficulties soon after and Dublin Corporation snapped it up for £3,500. The Round Room, designed by Francis Johnston, was added in 1821 for the visit of King George IV. In 1919 the first Irish Parliament, unrecognised by the British Government, adopted the Declaration of Independence in the Mansion House. It is not open to the public.

37. St Ann's Church
- Dawson Street

This church, while built in 1720 and retaining much of Isaac Wills' 18th century-interior, has lost its original exterior due to extensive renovation work by Thomas Deane in 1868. It now possesses a Victorian Romanesque facade and presents a fine view down Anne Street opposite. Near the altar there is a shelf which dates to 1723 and recalls an unusual bequest by the Right Hon. Theophilus Lord Newton that loaves of bread be left there every day for the poor people of Dublin. Today the church is noted for its lunchtime recitals.

North of the Liffey

As far back as the early 19th century, the north side of the city has been less fashionable than the south side. A result of this has been severe deterioration of some of the northside buildings, though it must be said that both sides of the city have suffered a lot in this regard. Many of the principal tourist attractions are on the south side (Trinity College, the cathedrals of St Patrick and Christ Church, Dublin Castle, the Guinness Brewery, the National Museum and National Gallery) but the north side has an authenticity which is indisputable. It also has the General Post Office (GPO), headquarters of the 1916 Easter Rising; it has two of the city's finest 18th-century public buildings, the Custom House and the Four Courts; and many more places of social, historical and architectural interest. (Numbers in brackets refer to other entries in *Things To See And Do*)

38. O'Connell Street (✔)

The Earl of Drogheda, Henry Moore, left his name all over this area of the city. Drogheda Street, Earl Street, Henry Street, Moore Street, and, believe it or not, Of Lane. In the 1720s Drogheda Street was a narrow stretch of road which led from a country road (now Parnell Street) to where the General Post Office (GPO) today stands. It became Gardiner's Mall in the 1740s, Sackville Street in 1758 when it was widened and lined with trees, and eventually, in 1924, O'Connell Street. Of Lane has disappeared, but Henry, Moore and Earl have survived and are today busy shopping streets off O'Connell Street.

The most significant building on the street is the GPO (**39**). It was here, on Easter Monday 1916, that the leaders of the Irish Volunteers read out the Proclamation of the Irish Republic and held out against the might of the British forces for almost a week. When they surrendered they formed a line on Moore Street and marched in file up Henry Street, past the blazing GPO and onto Drogheda (now O'Connell) Street where they laid down their arms. Eight houses were ablaze in Drogheda Street, over fifty in Henry Street, over thirty in Earl Street and about a dozen in Moore Street. Finally, they were marched to the Rotunda Hospital (**50**) where they spent the night on the lawn outside the hospital, watched over by British soldiers whose fixed bayonets

were directed towards the 400 prisoners. O'Connell Street suffered again in 1922 when, during the Civil War, many more buildings were destroyed. The street you see today is a result of major rebuilding in the 1920s. Two monuments dominate the street, one at each end. A third, a slender, steel needle rising high above the city, is planned for the Millennium and will stand on the central mall near the GPO. At the southern end, facing across the Liffey, is the impressive statue of Daniel O'Connell (1775-1847), the *Liberator* who fought through political and peaceful means for Catholic Emancipation. The seated, winged figures represent O'Connell's virtues of courage, eloquence, fidelity and patriotism. A breast of the seated figure on the south-east side has a clearly distinguishable bullet hole, a remnant of either the 1916 Rising or the 1922 Civil War. At the far end of the street is the imposing monument to Charles Stewart Parnell (1846-91). It was Parnell, the Protestant Member of Parliament, who fought through political means for the realisation of Home Rule. One of Ireland's cherished historical figures, he died at age forty-five, deposed by his party and scorned by a public who once thought he could do no wrong. This turn-around in his fortunes came about as a result of his exposed affair with a married woman, Kitty O'Shea, wife of a Captain O'Shea. Near the GPO is a statue of James Larkin, a trade union leader who organised a general strike in 1913, and between Parnell and Larkin is a statue commemorating the 'apostle of temperance', Father Theobald Mathew. Despite his dedication, a tour of Dublin pubs will testify to his dismal failure in a city devoted to the odd drink or two! Facing the GPO, at the top of North Earl Street, leans the bronze figure of a pensive James Joyce on his bronze cane. Were he alive today he would probably smile approvingly at the disrespectful Dubliner who nicknamed the 1988 Anna Livia fountain in the middle of O'Connell Street 'The Floozie in the Jacuzzi'.

39. General Post Office
- O'Connell Street

The GPO was the scene of the 1916 Easter Rising. Patrick Pearse, James Connolly and some of the other leaders of the Rising read the Proclamation of the Irish Republic from outside the building, before embarking on their badly organised and some would say foolhardy mission. Their untimely end was only a couple of weeks away, but the events which took place during the week that they occupied this building dramatically changed the course of Irish history. Built in 1818 to the design of Francis Johnston, the GPO might not have been built in this location had it not been for the Catholic authorities deciding that a Catholic cathedral in such a prominent site might generate too much Protestant hostility. Their Pro-Cathedral was subsequently built on Marlborough Street, and Francis Johnston was commissioned to design the General Post Office. The three statues on top of the building represent Hibernia, Mercury and Fidelity. A memorial to the Rising was recently moved to the central window on the ground floor for all passers-by to see. It is a bronze statue of the mythic Cuchulann, dying, with a raven on his shoulder. The words of the Proclamation of 1916 are imprinted on the statue's plinth, as are the names of its signatories. After the building was burnt out during the Rising, and further damaged during the 1922 Civil War, it remained closed until 1929. Today, the GPO still functions as the principal post office for Dublin city.

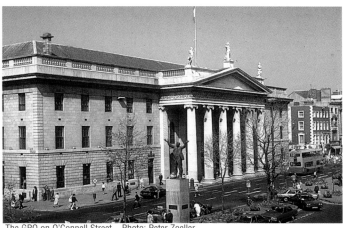

The GPO on O'Connell Street.   Photo: Peter Zoeller.

40. Pro-Cathedral
- Marlborough Street

This, the church of St Mary, is a very large building cramped on a narrow street and as such is the great unnoticed church in Dublin. It was built between 1815 and 1825 by a relatively unknown architect, John Sweetman. It would not be out of place on O'Connell Street, and indeed that was where this cathedral was originally to be built. Although a site was available - where now stands the GPO - the Catholic authorities decided against raising the ire of a Protestant community still very wary of the Catholic church. The Pro-Cathedral is sometimes used for State occasions and at different times of the year great church music accompanies the religious services. The area immediately north of the church was once known as 'Monto', a red-light district which featured in James Joyce's autobiographical novel, *A Portrait of the Artist as a Young Man*.

41. Tyrone House
- Marlborough Street

This 1740 house was designed by Richard Castle for Sir Marcus Beresford, Viscount and later Earl of Tyrone. It was an important house of the period and some of the interior plasterwork is by the skilled Francini brothers. The house was bought by the Government in 1835 and, partly altered, now houses a section of the Department of Education. The building is opposite the Pro-Cathedral and a 19th-century replica of the house was built almost beside it to the north, so be careful if you are taking a photograph not to snap the impostor. Incidentally, the replica was destroyed by fire in 1998 but has been rebuilt.

42. Abbey Theatre
- Marlborough Street

The Abbey Theatre was founded by Lady Gregory and W.B. Yeats and opened in 1904. Its first stormy controversy burst on stage in 1907 with the rioting which greeted J.M. Synge's *Playboy of the Western World*. The vaguely immoral tone which the play suggested shocked the puritan mind of the mainly Catholic and nationalist audience. Riots again erupted in 1926 when Seán O'Casey's passionate 1916 Easter Rising drama, *The Plough and the Stars*, disgusted the audience with its honest attempt to portray the drama of the Rising. In 1951 the building was destroyed by fire and in 1966 the present building, designed by Michael Scott, was opened. It is a bland building, despite recent attempts to dress it up. The main theatre seats over 600, while the underground Peacock Theatre seats 157. The main foyer has many interesting portraits of famous Irish theatrical figures.

43. Custom House (✔)
- Custom House Quay

The Custom House (1781-91) is widely regarded as Dublin's greatest 18th-century public building. It dominates the eastern Liffey quays and is best seen from the south bank of the river. To the 19th-century sea merchants arriving into Dublin for the first time, it presented a serenely imposing vista. The building is 114 m long, with a central Corinthian column and arcades on each side linking the end pavilions. The four statues on the roof represent Neptune, Mercury, Plenty and Industry. The building is topped by a copper dome above which stands a figure representing Hope. In 1990 the entire building was cleaned and some necessary restoration work was executed in

Custom House.   Photo: Peter Zoeller.

the process.

In 1921 the entire building was gutted by fire in the struggle for Independence, but it was later rebuilt with complete fidelity to the original. James Gandon, arguably the greatest architect ever to work in Dublin, designed the original Custom House and was frequently seen on the building site carrying a sword. This was on account of the extreme unpopularity of the building: local residents feared the area would become a slum, while merchants and traders in the Temple Bar area of the city - where the existing Custom House stood - feared for their livelihood. In fact, the new Custom House did help to transform the dynamic of the city because, only a few years after its completion, Carlisle (now O'Connell) Bridge was built and the city's axis shifted eastwards. The building today houses the Department of the Environment.

44. Mountjoy Square

It is said of Dublin's five Georgian squares that Mountjoy Square is the only actual square. It was built between 1792 and 1818 and for a time was called Gardiner Square,

after the master developer of the 18th century, Luke Gardiner. He became Viscount Mountjoy later in life, thus the name today. Mountjoy Square is at the top of the hill which rises gradually northwards from the Custom House. This connecting street today is dilapidated and parts of the area are like a wasteland, but in its day Gardiner Street was one of the most magnificent streets in Dublin. Today, Mountjoy Square shows the signs of an area left neglected for too long, though recent rebuilding has made the square more presentable. Fortunately, the houses on the east and north sides have survived the urban decay that affected the west and south sides. In 1014, Brian Boru is believed to have camped here during the Battle of Clontarf. Seán O'Casey, the playwright, lived at No. 35 and his play, *The Shadow of a Gunman*, is probably set here. In nearby Fitzgibbon Street, James Joyce spent some of his boyhood at No. 14.

45. St Francis Xavier Church
-   Upper Gardiner Street

The main reason for visiting this 1829-32 Catholic church is to view the splendid Italian high altar,

unique in Dublin, and the majesty
coffered ceiling. The church was
designed by J.B. Keane (not to be
mistaken for the Kerry playwright,
alive and well in his home town of
Listowel) and is featured at the end
of James Joyce's short story,
Grace.

46. St George's Church - Temple Street
North/Hardwicke Place

The celebrated architect Francis
Johnston designed St George's
Church and it was completed in
1802. Many regard it as Johnston's
finest work, although it is
impossible to appreciate it fully as
it is no longer in use. Nonetheless,
one can still admire the building's
facade and rising spire whose top
is almost 200 feet from the ground.
Inside there is a great feeling of
space, with interesting stained-
glass windows by Evie Hone. The
bells were added in 1836 after
neighbours of Johnston, who lived
in No. 64 Eccles Street,
complained about the noise they
made: Johnston, a lover of bells,
had had them installed in a
purpose-built bell-tower in his
back garden! He donated them to
St George's. The Duke of
Wellington was married in this
church.

47. James Joyce Cultural Centre - 35 North Great George's Street

North Great George's Street has
largely survived the urban decay
which beset much of north
Dublin's 18th-century building
stock. During the early 19th
century, there was a large, iron
gate at the bottom of the street and
this, mirrored at the top by the fine
Belvedere House, gave the street a
private and exclusive atmosphere.
Today, many of the houses are
occupied by committed
conservationists who are

painstakingly restoring them to
their original condition.
One of these houses, No. 35, was
opened in 1994 as a cultural centre
for students and admirers of James
Joyce. The Joycean scholar,
Senator David Norris, has been
one of the driving forces behind
this exciting project. The street
dates from around 1775.
Opening Hours: Open Mon-Sat
09.30-17.00. Sun 12.30-17.00.
Guided tours throughout the day.
Joycean walks from the Centre.
Tel: (01) 8788547.

48. Belvedere House - Great Denmark Street

Lord Belvedere's house was begun
in 1775 and is today occupied by a
Jesuit school for boys, Belvedere
College. Fortunately, when the
school bought the house in 1841,
they left intact the beautiful Apollo
and Diana Rooms, which have
splendid plasterwork by Michael
Stapleton. Regrettably, the central
part of Stapleton's ceiling in the
Venus Room was removed. The
fireplaces, by the Venetian, Bossi,
are among the finest in Dublin.
James Joyce attended school here
between 1893 and 1898, and it is
featured in his *A Portrait of the
Artist as a Young Man.* Not open
to the public.

49. Parnell Square

Parnell Square was the second
Georgian square to be laid out,
after St Stephen's Green.
Originally called Rutland Square,
the northern terrace was laid out in
1755 and seven years later Lord
Charlemont bought this land and
built his mansion, Charlemont
House, now the Municipal Gallery
of Modern Art (**51**). During the
Square's development period the
altruistic and charitable
Bartholomew Mosse was putting
into motion his plans for the
building of a maternity hospital on
the south side of the Square. This

was to become known as Dr Mosse's Lying-In Hospital, now the Rotunda (**50**). The east side of the Square is the home of the Gate Theatre (**53**). Oliver St John Gogarty, a contemporary of James Joyce, was born at No. 5 in 1878. The character of Buck Mulligan in *Ulysses* is based on Gogarty. On the north side is the **Garden of Remembrance**, laid out in 1966 to commemorate the 1916 Easter Rising as well as all Irish soldiers who fell in all civil and other wars. The statue, by Oisín Kelly, at the end of the Garden represents the *Children of Lir* who, in one of Ireland's most arresting legends, were turned into swans for 900 years. Almost beside Charlemont House is the newly-established Dublin Writers Museum (**52**). The church with the slender spire on the north-east corner of the Square was built in 1864 with money provided by a well-known, Scottish-born brewer and grocer, Alex Findlater. He had established significant business interests in the city and the church is to this day known as 'Findlater's Church'.

On nearby Granby Row, north of Parnell Square, is the **National Wax Museum** *Tel: 01-8726340.* It is open Mon-Sat 10.00-17.30 and Sun 12.00-17.30. Admission: Adults £3.50, Senior Citizens/Students £2.50, Children £2. There are life-size replicas of Irish political and cultural figures, as well as many contemporary personalities.

50. Rotunda Hospital
- Parnell Square

The Rotunda Hospital is the oldest maternity hospital in the world. Its founder, Dr Bartholomew Mosse, founded his first maternity hospital on 15 March 1745 in George's Lane, now South Great George's Street, and opposite Fade Street, but soon the tiny hospital had achieved such a reputation that by 1750 Mosse commissioned his friend and architect, Richard

Castle, to design a large hospital on Parnell Street. Castle, aware of the good doctor's financial constraints, used his earlier Leinster House design as the blueprint for the new building and by 1757 the magnificent Lying-In Hospital had opened its doors, doors which were principally used by the poverty-stricken, pregnant women of Dublin. To raise money, Mosse converted the grounds behind the hospital into the most elegant of private gardens to which Lords, Ladies, Dukes, Earls and Members of Parliament flocked. The Rotunda Gardens were to become the aristocratic amusement grounds of the city. The Square surrounding the hospital and gardens housed, in 1792, eleven peers, two bishops and eleven Members of Parliament.

Nothing remains of these wonderful Gardens today because of the Hospital's expansion over the years, extending today as far as the Garden of Remembrance. The adjoining Rotunda building was built after Mosse's death, as were the New Assembly Rooms, now the Gate Theatre. One of the most remarkable interiors in Dublin is that of the Rotunda Chapel, completed in 1758 and with stunning plasterwork throughout, executed by Bartholomew Cramillion.

Bartholomew Mosse is buried in an unknown grave in the Dublin suburb of Donnybrook. His remarkable contribution in taking Dublin out of the Dark Ages of high childbirth mortality was only fully recognised almost a century after his death when Sir William Wilde published a paper on his extraordinary achievements.

51. Hugh Lane Municipal Gallery of Modern Art
- Parnell Square

The well-known architect of the day, William Chambers, designed Charlemont House (1762-5) on the north side of Parnell Square for the

Earl of Charlemont. In 1927 the Irish Government presented the house to the city. Dublin Corporation undertook the renovation, adapting the interior for use as an art gallery. The Hugh Lane Municipal Gallery of Modern Art was opened in 1933, named after the man who was a patron of the arts until he died tragically in the 1915 sinking of the Lusitania. Because of a dispute between the London Tate Gallery and the Municipal Gallery, interminable negotiations took place over which Gallery would exhibit the Hugh Lane Bequest. An agreement was reached in 1959 and the present agreement of 1994 decrees that twenty-seven of the paintings remain on loan in Dublin, while a further eight will move between the National Gallery in London and Dublin. This agreement will last for fourteen years.
Opening Hours: Tues-Thurs 9.30-18.00. Fri/Sat 9.30-17.00. Sun 11.00-17.00. Closed Mon. Admission: Free.

Hugh Lane Municipal Gallery of Modern Art. Photo: Peter Zoeller.

Tel: (01) 8741903/4
There is a Gallery restaurant open for morning coffee, lunches and afternoon tea.

52. Dublin Writers Museum - Parnell Square

Beside the Hugh Lane Gallery at the top of Parnell Square is the Dublin Writers Museum. It opened to the public in 1991 as part of Dublin's celebrations as European City of Culture. Collections of rare editions, manuscript items and memorabilia relating to the great Irish writers live within a beautifully restored 18th-century townhouse. There are also temporary exhibition rooms, a library of rare books, a splendid gallery of portraits and busts, a fine bookshop and areas for lectures and readings. In adjoining No. 19, the Irish Writers Centre offers a setting in which writers can meet, talk and work.
Opening Hours: Mid-Mar-31 Oct: Mon-Sat 10.00-17.00, Sun 11.30-18.00. Nov-mid-Mar: Telephone for details. Admission: Adults £3, Senior Citizens/Students/Under 18s £2.55, Children £1.40. Tours are available in foreign languages.
Tel: (01) 8722077
There is a café and bookshop at the back of the house and a restaurant, *Chapter One*, in the basement.

53. Gate Theatre - Parnell Square/Cavendish Row

The Gate Theatre Company was established by Micheál MacLiammóir and Hilton Edwards and performed its first play in the present theatre in 1929. This was Oscar Wilde's *Salomé*, which in 1993 played to packed houses in the same theatre in a stunning production by Stephen Berkoff. MacLiammóir was possibly Ireland's greatest actor. He was famous for his one-man show, *The Importance of Being Oscar*, which he played up to 1975 when he was 76 years of age. Orson Welles was a friend of MacLiammóir and Edwards and he gained early acting experience on the Gate's boards, as did James Mason. For many years Lord Longford was associated with the theatre. A photograph displayed on the walls inside shows him outside the theatre with a collection box during some of the Gate's most difficult years.

Built between 1784-6 as the New Assembly Rooms, they were part of the overall strategy to raise continuous funds for the Rotunda Hospital. Today the Gate is a vital component of the Dublin theatre scene.

54. Moore Street

Immediately west of the Rotunda Hospital is a colourful and busy open market street. This is where Dublin traders have traded from open stalls through generations of families. The traders are friendly, but you will not find them easy to haggle with as they are not accustomed to giving an inch. The street itself has important historical connections. It was once the home of 'The Dublin Infirmary for Curing Diseases of the Skin', the first hospital of its kind in the British Dominions. It was located at No. 20, opened in 1818, and closed in 1837 due to financial difficulties, but not before having dealt with 22,000 patients. The street has always been associated with a rich variety of trades and even during the Irish Famine (1845-8) there were 62 shops, 41 of which were dealing in food of one variety or another, and a further 9 were butcher shops. However, it was through the events of the 1916 Easter Rising that Moore Street truly stepped into Irish history, for it was at the north end of the street, where it meets Parnell Street, that Patrick Pearse surrendered to the British Commanding Officer, General Lowe, at the end of the fighting. It was in Plunkett's fish and poultry shop on Moore Street where the final meeting of the Irish Volunteers' command took place and where the decision to lay down arms was reached. And it was on Moore Street that the surrendering Volunteers formed a line and marched, flanked by two soldiers with white flags, up Henry Place and onto O'Connell Street to lay down their arms. The west side of modern Moore Street was largely demolished to make way for the ILAC Shopping Centre in the 1970s.

55. King's Inns and Henrietta Street

A detour to nearby Henrietta Street and the King's Inns is well worth the trouble. The King's Inns is the home of the legal profession. The building was designed by James Gandon and was begun in 1795. However, it took until 1817 to complete, by which time other architects had become involved, among them Francis Johnston. You can approach the building from Constitution Hill, or from Henrietta Street. The interior of the building is not easily seen as its use is for members of the King's Inns only. Nevertheless, it is worth your while to go slightly out of your way to see it, especially from the park at the Constitution Hill side, but also to take in on your way back the earliest of all the Georgian streets, Henrietta Street (from 1720). Today, the houses are in very poor condition, but they are particularly fine examples of early Georgian townhouses. If this street is ever given the attention - and the money - it so richly deserves, it would undoubtedly become again one of Dublin's most elegant streets. The developer, Luke Gardiner, lived at No. 10, and the street was for a time called locally *Primate's Hill* because of the many senior clergy and at least one archbishop who lived here.

56. St Mary's Church - Mary Street

St Mary's Church stands at the end of Wolfe Tone Park, at the corner of Mary Street and Jervis Street.

The park was formerly the church's cemetery. St Mary's was designed by Thomas Burgh in 1697 and completed in 1702. During the 18th century it was Dublin's most fashionable church. Arthur Guinness married Ann Lee here in 1793. A host of famous Irishmen were baptised here, among them the Earl of Charlemont in 1728, the writer Richard Brinsley Sheridan in 1751, the patriot Theobald Wolfe Tone in 1763 (he was born in nearby Wolfe Tone Street), the celebrated mathematician Sir William Rowan Hamilton in 1805, and the playwright Seán O'Casey in 1880. In its new life, the building now dispenses food and drink instead of religion.

57. St Mary's Abbey
- Meetinghouse Lane

Branching west off Capel Street is a small street called Mary's Abbey. This is where you go to find the 1180 chapter-house remains of the 12th-century Cistercian St Mary's Abbey, one of the most important monasteries in Ireland until its dissolution in 1537 by Henry VIII. The chapter-house is where the monks used to gather after mass. It is 2 m below ground level, evidence that the city has risen through building and rebuilding over the centuries. At the height of its influence St Mary's Abbey was the wealthiest monastery in Ireland. Its land stretched to modern day Ballybough to the east, while its cemetery was situated around the Green Street/North King Street area of the city. The chapter-house was also used for political meetings and in 1534 Lord Silken Thomas Fitzgerald renounced his allegiance to Henry VIII in this building. His rebellion was short lived and he was executed soon after at Tyburn. The chapter-house remains are worth going to see, however opening times often prove simply too restrictive for

visitors to the city.
Opening Hours: mid-June - mid-Sept: Wed only 10.00-17.00. Admission: Adults £1.00, Senior Citizens 70p, Students/Children 40p. *Tel: (01) 8721490*

58. St Michan's Church
- Lower Church Street

St Michan was a Danish bishop and this church was founded in Dublin at a time when Dublin wasn't short of Danes. The church's foundation dates to 1095, however numerous restorations and rebuildings took place over the centuries, especially in 1686, and again after the 1922 Civil War. The church's main attraction for visitors has nothing to do with religion or with its fine architecture. The church vaults possess a rarefied atmosphere which has kept some unfortunate corpses in a semi-mummified condition. Some years ago it was possible to shake the hands of some of the corpses. Happily, that weird and eerie practice is no longer allowed. In 1742, the year when Handel played the first *Messiah* in the Old Music Hall in Fishamble Street, he used the present organ in St Michan's on which to practise. You can see the original keyboard in the display area of the church.
Opening Hours: Mon-Fri 10.00-12.45 and 14.00-16.45. Sat 10.00-12.45. Sun Services 10.00. There are regular tours of the church. Admission: Adults £1.20, Children 50p. *Tel: (01) 8724154*

59. Old Jameson Distillery
- Bow Street

Around the corner from St Michan's Church is an old warehouse on Bow Street which has been converted by Irish Distillers into a museum. Jameson Whiskey has been distilled here

since 1780. The Jameson family built up the company to become one of the largest in Ireland. In 1966, a merger of John Jameson & Son, John Power & Son and Cork Distilleries Company brought about a new whiskey conglomerate, Irish Distillers. Bushmills Distillery in County Antrim joined the Irish Distillers Group in 1972. The present Visitor Centre, a carefully constructed replica of a living distillery, opened to the public in 1997. It replaced the Irish Whiskey Corner. The hour-long tour begins with an eight-minute multilingual, audio-visual presentation on Jameson Whiskey. This is followed by a guided tour of the recreated distillery and covers the malting, milling and mashing of barley, followed by fermentation, distillation, vatting and bottling. Appropriately, the tour ends in the new Jameson Bar, with a glass of Jameson. If you offer yourself up as a 'taster', not only will you get a chance to taste several different whiskeys, you will also receive a nicely produced certificate, stating that you are 'a qualified Irish Whiskey Taster'. All in all, a thoroughly enjoyable visit.
Opening Hours: Every day 09.30 last tour 17.30. Tours throughout the day. Admission: Adults £3.95, Senior Citizens £3, Children £1.50, Family £9.50.
Tel: (01) 8072355

60. Four Courts
- Inns Quay

The Four Courts is the home of the Irish Law Courts, and what a fine home they have. Designed by James Gandon (Custom House) and begun in 1786, it was not completed until 1802. This was partly because Gandon, fearing civil strife towards the end of the century, returned to England for a period. In 1922, after the signing of the Anglo-Irish Treaty in 1921, anti-Treaty forces occupied the Four Courts building. Michael Collins, increasingly seen as a hero of Irish history, wrought widespread destruction on the building when he ordered it to be shelled from across the Liffey. The building went up in flames, destroying for ever important early historical records. In 1932 the building was rebuilt with complete deference to the original, except for the central dome which is too high. Nevertheless, the present building is a magnificent work by Gandon, stretching as it does along the Liffey for 130 m. The large, central Corinthian block is joined on each side by a courtyard with open arcades facing onto the quayside, and these courtyards are further joined by the two end wings of the complex.

The Four Courts stands on the former site of a 1224 Dominican foundation, the Abbey of St Saviour. Stones from this demolished abbey were used to build two of old Dublin's fortified stone gates, that of St Audoen and

Four Courts. Photo: Bord Fáilte.

Winetavern Street. Some of these stones are today in the wall around St Audoen's Gate on Cook Street. Just above the Four Courts is Father Mathew Bridge, the location of Áth Cliath (ford of the hurdles) where the Vikings formed the first bridging of the Liffey in the 9th century, and from where the Irish name for Dublin, Baile Átha Cliath, has its origin.

Best of the Rest

Some of the places in this section are within walking distance, but most are a little too far for the casual walker. All are accessible by public transport. For all bus information telephone (01) 8734222, and for train information, including the DART (Dublin Area Rapid Transport), telephone (01) 8366222.

Phoenix Park

The Phoenix Park is the largest enclosed urban park in Europe, the circumference being 11.2 km and the encircling walls covering an area of 1,752 acres (over 700 hectares). It was first enclosed by the Duke of Ormond in 1662 and opened as a public park in 1747. Although the park is public, there is a number of residences which are very strictly private. One of these is Áras an Uachtaráin (House of the President). The house was built in 1751, was added onto in 1782 and in 1816 the celebrated architect Francis Johnston added the Ionic portico. Between 1782 and 1922 the house was known as the Viceregal Lodge and was used as a residence for the Viceroy and lords lieutenant. When the office of

Phoenix Park. Photo: Peter Zoeller.

President was created in 1937 it became the official residence of the President of the Irish Republic, which is a seven-year term. Another house which has an official use is the residence of the American Ambassador. It was formerly the Chief Secretary's Lodge and Demesne.
Two very fine monuments are in the Phoenix Park. Entering via

Parkgate Street you will come upon a 63 m high obelisk which you cannot really miss. This is the Wellington Monument (1817-61) which commemorates Arthur Wellesley, Duke of Wellington. There is a dispute over Wellesley's birthplace which was either near Trim, Co. Meath or at 24 Merrion Street Upper, opposite Government Buildings. Mid-way up the main road which dissects the park you will pass on your right Áras an Uachtaráin and a little further on in the middle of the road, the Phoenix Monument, erected by Lord Chesterfield in 1747. (It is believed the name of the park derives from the old Gaelic words for clear water - Fionn Uisce - and not from the legend of the phoenix rising from the ashes.) The American Ambassador's residence is directly to the left of the Phoenix Monument.
The Phoenix Park is the lungs of the city, with its numerous trees and large, open, grassy spaces. Its many sporting facilities - over forty soccer pitches, the second oldest cricket club in Ireland (Trinity Cricket Club is the oldest), a vast training ground for budding athletes and for ordinary Joe and Mary Citizen trying to keep fit - provide an amenity that is only partly understood and appreciated by the vast majority of Dubliners. Dublin Zoo, one of the world's oldest zoos, is also located here. A word of caution. There has been an increase in petty crime in the Park in recent years so, as a precaution, visit with a companion if you can and leave your valuables and money in your hotel or guesthouse.
How to get there: Walk up the north side of the Liffey Quays and, passing the famous Ryan's pub on Parkgate Street, enter the Park through the main gates ahead of you. Buses 10/25/25A/26/51/51B/66/66A/67/67A from the city

centre. If you want to get a bus to the far end of the Park and walk through it and back to the city, catch the No. 37 from Lower Abbey Street and get off at the Castleknock Gates.

Phoenix Park Visitor Centre:
An historical interpretation of the past from 3500 BC to the present day with exhibitions, a film show and restaurant. *Tel: (01) 6770095* for opening times. Admission: Adults £2, Groups/Senior Citizens £1.50, Children/Students £1, Family £5.

Dublin Canals

The two Canals of Dublin, the Grand and the Royal, were built in the 18th century to provide inland waterway access from Dublin to the River Shannon and to the midlands of the country.

They have for a long time been regarded as a sort of inner-city boundary and today are an attractive feature of the city, providing, on some stretches of the water, a beautiful environment for walking.

The Grand Canal

The construction of the Grand Canal began in 1756 to connect Dublin with Ireland's longest river, the Shannon, thereby creating an inland waterway transport route to the west of the country. When completed in 1796 it was the longest stretch of canal in the British Isles, 550 km in total when combined with the Shannon and Barrow rivers. There were five hotels built along the Canal between Dublin and the Shannon to cater for the passengers who were an important source of revenue for the Canal Company. However it was in the transportation of cargo that the greatest source of revenue was derived. The barges were pulled by horses and some of them travelled at speeds of up to 15 km/h. With the advent of railway travel from the 1850s the Canal began a decline from which it could never

Grand Canal.   Photo: Peter Zoeller.

recover and it was closed to commercial traffic in 1960.

From Ringsend, where it connects with the Liffey, the Grand Canal curves westwards across the often leafy southern suburbs of the city. It is possible to walk along the ancient towpath for much of the route and a particularly interesting stretch is between Leeson Street and Lower Mount Street. It was in this area of the city that the poet Patrick Kavanagh spent much of his time and there is a bronze memorial to him on the Canal banks near Baggot Street Bridge (mind you don't sit on his hat!). Another interesting part of the Canal is at Portobello Bridge, where Portobello House, built in 1807, recalls its original use as Portobello Hotel, a busy terminus hotel in the early 1800s. The Canal has been neglected over the years, but there are plans to restore it to its former glory. An interesting fact is that all the locks have been kept in working order.

Waterways Visitor Centre

The centre houses an exhibition which explores Ireland's inland waterways, their historical background and their modern amenity uses. The exhibitions are imaginatively presented and the information easy to absorb.

Opening Hours: Open all year round. Jun-Sept 09.30-18.30 seven days a week. Oct-May Wed-Sun 12.30-17.00 . Admission: Adults £2, Senior Citizens/Groups £1.50, Students/Children £1, Family £5. *Tel: (01) 6777510*
How to get there: Walk away from the city centre to the end of Pearse Street and you will see it in the water to your right. Bus No. 3 from O'Connell Street or outside Screen Cinema.

The Royal Canal

The Royal Canal Company was founded in 1789 by Long John Binns, his intention being to construct a northside rival to the Grand Canal which ran through the south side of the city. It was never a serious rival to the Grand Canal, largely because its route duplicated that of the Grand, but also because, by the time it was operational, the passenger trade along the Grand was already declining. In 1840 the Canal was sold to a railway company which proceeded to build a line along its banks, from Dublin to Mullingar.
As with the Grand, you can walk along the towpath of much of the Royal Canal, beginning at Newcomen Bridge, just north of Connolly Station, and walking westwards as far as you like. It is currently undergoing restoration with a view to creating a leisure and tourism amenity along its route.

National Botanic Gardens - Glasnevin

These Gardens were established in 1795 and cover an area of approximately nineteen hectares. For the horticulturist and botanist the Gardens are an important source of reference, but for most Dubliners it is simply a pleasant place to go on a Sunday afternoon for a tranquil stroll, while marvelling at some of the 20,000 species of flora growing within the confines of the Gardens. The best time of the year to visit is late spring and summer, but even during the winter there is plenty to see thanks to the fine Curvilinear Range of glasshouses which are an

Botanic Gardens, Glasnevin.
Photo: Peter Zoeller.

architectural feature of the Gardens. These glasshouses date to 1843 and are among the oldest glass conservatories in the world. The Yew Walk was planted fifty years before the Gardens opened and contains the oldest trees within the complex
Opening Hours: Summer: Mon-Sat 09.00-18.00. Sun 11.00-18.00. Winter: Mon-Sat 10.00-16.30. Sun 11.00-16.30. Admission: Free. *Tel: (01) 8377596/8374388*
How to get there: Bus No. 13 or 19 from O'Connell Street or No. 34/34A from Middle Abbey Street.

Prospect Cemetery
- Glasnevin

Prospect, or Glasnevin, Cemetery is Ireland's largest cemetery at over fifty hectares. It possesses an enormous variety of headstones dating back to its establishment in 1832 as a burial place for Catholics. At that time Catholic families were experiencing grave (!) difficulties in trying to bury their loved ones elsewhere in Dublin. The cemetery is full of monuments with strong nationalist images and indeed many famous patriots are buried here. The older part of the cemetery is surrounded by high stone walls with small watchtowers. These were built to keep down the epidemic of body-snatching in the early 19th century. Daniel O'Connell 'the Liberator' founded the cemetery and he is buried near the O'Connell Monument, the 51 m high granite round tower at the main gates. O'Connell died in 1847 and was reinterred in 1869, the same year the round tower was completed. A long list of famous Irish men and women are buried in the cemetery, among them politicians, writers, actors, artists and academics. Charles Stewart Parnell is buried here, his tomb weighed down by a huge granite boulder from his Avondale estate. Roger Casement, Michael Collins, Éamon de Valera, Countess Markievicz, Gerard Manley Hopkins, Brendan Behan - just some of the illustrious names whose remains are to be found in different parts of the cemetery. You could spend a day here, but a couple of hours will allow you see the most interesting part of the cemetery which is in the old, Prospect Square end.
Opening Hours: Daily 08.00-17.00 (16.30 Nov-Jan) Admission: Free. *Tel: (01) 8301133.* The National Graves Association organises tours of the cemetery. The tours concentrate on the political and Republican memorials.
How to get there: Buses 13/19/19A/40/40A from city centre.

Casino at Marino
- Malahide Road

This unique architectural folly was designed by the celebrated architect William Chambers (Chapel and Examination Hall in Trinity, Municipal Gallery on Parnell Square) in 1758 for Lord Charlemont who had just returned, at the age of twenty-seven, from a nine-year trip to Europe, possessing an enormous art collection together with grand ideas for his estate in Marino. The building is an extraordinary *coup d'oeil*. The exterior, with its twelve Tuscan columns and large doorway, creates the idea of a symmetrical, one-roomed Palladian-style villa. Once inside all these simple expectations disappear as you realise that the interior is a complex structure within which are found rooms of varying sizes on different levels. Lord Charlemont intended it to be used as a bachelor residence but after his marriage it became a garden retreat instead. In 1870 his Parnell Square townhouse was sold to the government, and by 1930 his Marino Estate and the Casino had all been sold. The Casino has been completely restored and despite the poor geographical aspect it enjoys today, surrounded as it is by a housing estate, it is one of Dublin's most intriguing buildings. The nearby Marino Crescent which faces on to the sea was built in 1792. Here, in No. 15, Bram Stoker, creator of Dracula, was born in 1847.
Opening Hours: June-Sept: daily 09.30-18.30. Oct: daily 10.00-17.00. Nov and Feb-Apr: Sun and Thurs 12.00-16.00. Admission, which includes a guided tour: Adults £2, Senior Citizens/Groups £1.50, Students/Children £1, Family £5.
Tel: (01) 6613111 ext. 2386
How to get there: Buses 20A/20B/27/27A/27B/32A/42/42B - all from the city centre.

Drimnagh Castle

Drimnagh Castle, opened to the public in 1991, is a recently restored medieval castle with 17th-century French-style gardens and enclosed by a fully flooded moat. Built between 1220 and 1250, it houses the only authentically restored medieval Great Hall in Dublin. A replica tiled floor, timber minstrels' gallery, oak roof constructed by hand and hand-carved effigies of site workers in period dress all combine to recreate the atmosphere of a 13th-century Irish castle.

Opening Hours: April-Sept: Wed/Sat/Sun 12.00-17.00. Oct-Mar: Sun only 14.00-17.00. Other days by appointment.
Tel: (01) 4502530. Admission, which includes a guided tour: Adults £1.50, Senior Citizens/Students/Group rate £1, Children 50p.

Ballsbridge

Ballsbridge is a largely 19th-century suburban development just outside the inner-city Grand Canal boundary. It has an impressive variety of large-scale red-brick houses, many of them now the home of small businesses. The greater number of the capital's embassies are in this area, as is a significant proportion of the city's semi-upmarket guesthouses and hotels.

When the Pembroke district area was being laid out, the plan was to extend the existing artery from Fitzwilliam Street/Fitzwilliam Square up Baggot Street to the Canal and further south into a new street which was to be named Pembroke Road. Pembroke Road in 1837 boasted the longest uninterrupted classical terrace in the city. The 700 m long Waterloo Road, with its set-back houses, was laid out in the 1840s at right angles to Pembroke Road and, in the 1850s, the tree-lined and exclusive Wellington and Raglan Roads were laid out parallel to Waterloo Road,

dissected by Elgin Road. This estate, the creation of Lord Pembroke, was a major planning and architectural achievement and to this day remains largely intact. It is a graceful and spacious area of the city and can be toured easily on foot. It marks the final phase in Dublin's great physical expansion before the 20th-century planners and architects lost sight of any further large-scale and cohesive development for the city.

Royal Dublin Society
- Merrion Road

The RDS, as it is known, was founded as the Dublin Society in 1731 to promote agriculture, the arts and science. Its first home was in the old Parliament House on College Green. Its longest residence was in Leinster House, from 1814 until the Free State government moved in in 1922. It has been in Ballsbridge ever since. During its influential existence it has been involved in the foundation of many cultural institutions, not least the National Museum, Library and Gallery. The principal show which is associated with the RDS is the annual Horse Show in early August (*see Calendar of Events*). The Show is Ireland's most important equestrian event with international competitors and significant prize money. There is a full calendar of business and leisure fairs throughout the year, and the adjoining Simmonscourt building frequently plays host to some of the biggest names in the music industry.

How to get there: Buses 5/7/7A/8, all from city centre. Five-minute walk from Sandymount DART Station.

Chester Beatty Library & Gallery of Oriental Art
- Dublin Castle

Sir Alfred Chester Beatty (1875-1968) was a mining engineer who, over the course of his lifetime,

The Horse Show at the Royal Dublin Society (RDS).
Photo: Peter Zoeller.

Rathfarnham Castle

Dating from c. 1590, the castle contains impressive 18th-century apartments designed by Sir William Chambers and James 'Athenian' Stuart for Henry Loftus, who had inherited the castle in the late 18th century. By the early 1900s, the castle was in ruins and the grounds completely overgrown. The current restoration has been under way since 1987.
Opening Hours: Jun-Sept: daily 10.00-18.00. Oct: daily 10.00-17.00. Access by guided tour only. Admission: Adult £1.50, Senior Citizens £1, Students/Children 60p, Family £4. *Tel: (01) 4939462 (6613111 out of season)*
How to get there: Buses 16/16A/17/47/47A/47B/75.

assembled large wealth and an extraordinary collection of valuable objects from the Middle and Far East in particular, but also a fine collection of Japanese prints and a priceless collection of medieval French books. For anyone interested in Oriental Art, this is an exceptional collection. The library and gallery moved recently to its new home in the castle grounds.
Opening Hours: Tues-Fri 10.00-17.00. Sat 14.00-17.00. Admission: Free. There are guided tours every Wed and Sat at 14.30.
Tel: (01) 2692386

George Bernard Shaw House   -   33 Synge Street

Near the Grand Canal Bridge at Portobello, this was Shaw's birthplace and his first home. Recently restored and opened to the public, the house is an interesting example of a domestic Victorian house and contains memorabilia relating to Shaw's life and work.
Opening Hours: May-Oct: Mon-Sat 10.00-17.00. Sun & Holidays 11.00-17.00. Closed for lunch 13.00-14.00. Nov-Apr: open by prior arrangement only. Admission: Adults £2.60, Senior Citizens/Students £2.10, Children £1.30, Family £7.75, *Tel: (01) 4750854 (8722077 out of season)*
How to get there: Buses 16/19/22 from city centre.

Pearse Museum
- St Enda's Park, Rathfarnham

A museum dedicated to the memory of Patrick Pearse (1879-1916), nationalist and educationalist who ran a school here from 1910 to 1916, the year he was executed for his part in the Easter Rising.
Opening Hours: Daily. May-Aug: 10.00-17.30. Sept-Oct: 10.00-17.00. Nov-Jan: 10.00-16.00. Feb-Apr: 10.00-17.00. Closed from 13.00 to 14.00. Admission: Free. Guided tour on request.
Tel: (01) 4934208
How to get there: Bus 16 from city centre.

A Walking Tour of 18th-Century Dublin

While Dublin's architecture is a mixture of styles from many different periods, what holds the city together and makes it a significant European city in terms of its buildings is the 18th-century planning and building legacy which graces the city today. The aristocracy in Dublin in the 18th century were an extremely powerful force in the political, cultural and social life of the city. In their own way they were far more powerful than their counterparts in London.

The dominant building material in Dublin is brick. This is certainly true of all the Georgian squares, but not so true of the most important buildings of the period. The great public buildings were of stone (Custom House, Four Courts, Bank of Ireland), as were many of the finest individual town mansions (Leinster House, Powerscourt House, Newman House, Charlemont House). The typical 18th-century terraced townhouse is a standard structure, four storeys high above a basement, three bays wide, and built in red brick. This general rule is true for St Stephen's Green, Merrion, Parnell and Mountjoy Squares. In contrast, Fitzwilliam Square, the latest of the squares, is smaller in scale, the houses here usually having only two bays.

The tour you are about to embark on will take you the best part of a day, more if you visit some of the buildings as you will surely wish to do. You can do the tour as it is written, or you can do it in reverse, and you can leave out places along the way. Places you should visit are indicated with (✔). The numbers in brackets refer to the *Things To See And Do* section and you should consult these entries for more information.

The Tour

Our tour begins at **Newman House(24) (✔)** on the southern side of St Stephen's Green. No. 85 was designed by Richard Castle in 1739 and the celebrated Francini brothers carved the superb plasterwork in the house. Their Apollo Room stands out as among the very finest in Dublin. No. 86 was built in 1765 to the design of Robert West. Both houses were acquired in 1865 by the Catholic University of Ireland.

Across the road and inside the railings of St Stephen's Green, facing

Typical Georgian Doors. Photo: Peter Zoeller.

Newman House, is a fine bronze bust of James Joyce. We stay on the south side of the Green and turn right and walk east past **Iveagh House (25),** once a fine Georgian residence and now the home of the Department of Foreign Affairs. At the bottom of Leeson Street look to your right up Earlsfort Terrace to the National Concert Hall, originally University College Dublin (UCD), recently restored and now Ireland's premier venue for classical concerts. The three pubs near the St Stephen's Green corner were once populated with students from nearby UCD (now in the suburbs). Going up Leeson Street, the Catholic University School on the left is a fine example of a restored Georgian

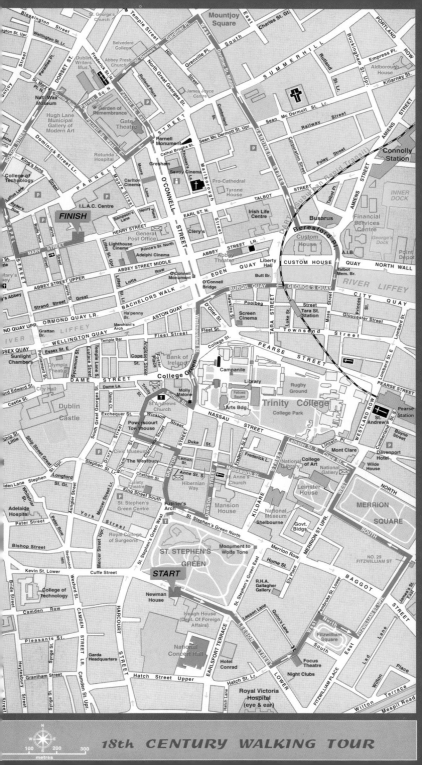

18th CENTURY WALKING TOUR

house. Before turning left into Pembroke Street take a look up the innocent-looking line of Georgian houses ahead. After midnight, the basements of many of these buildings open as nightclubs forming what is colloquially known as 'The Strip'. The glory days of these nightclubs has passed, but they still attract large numbers at weekends. If you come back at night, a word of advice. Go easy on the wine - it's not the best quality and is astronomically priced!

We go down Pembroke Street and onto **Fitzwilliam Square(26)**, the last, and smallest of Dublin's five Georgian squares. Note the fine doorways and overall excellent repair of the buildings which nowadays are almost exclusively used as offices. The medical profession has had associations with this Square for over a century. The park is not open to the public. Walking around two sides of the Square, keeping the park on your right, turn left into Fitzwilliam Street. Cross the intersection with Baggot Street and continue to **No. 29 Lower Fitzwilliam Street(27)(✔)** on your right. This is an impressively restored Georgian house, complete with period furniture and is open to the public. Guided tours are available which will help you more fully to appreciate the architecture, furnishings and lifestyle of the period. You are now at the south-east corner of **Merrion Square(28)**. Laid out from 1764 by John Ensor, this is a magnificent Georgian square, with four-storey-over-basement houses, three bays wide, all in an excellent state of repair. At the north-east corner the imposing Holles Street Maternity Hospital closes off the Square, while the west side is dominated by the **National Gallery(29)(✔)**, **Leinster Lawn** with **Leinster House(32)** in the background, and the **Natural History Museum(30)**. The park is open to the public and from it there is a fine view of the top two storeys of the

Molly Malone.
Photo: Peter Zoeller.

surrounding houses. Walk along the footpath outside the houses, looking out for commemorative plaques to some of the houses' famous past occupants.

Leave Merrion Square by the north-west corner, down from the National Gallery. The house on the opposite corner, No. 1 Merrion Square, was the home of Oscar Wilde who grew up here with his father, Sir William Wilde, and his mother, Lady Constance Wilde. View the flamboyant statue of Oscar directly opposite the house, inside the Square's railings. Oscar was born in nearby Westland Row, at No. 21. Go down Clare Street, passing on your left two of Dublin's most interesting shopfronts - Greene's Bookshop and Price's Medical Hall. Ahead of you is the long stretch of Nassau Street with the railings of Trinity College running along the right-hand side. Look up at the gable end of the last red-brick building before the railings. You will see the faint but distinct 'Finn's Hotel' marked on the side wall, advertising the fact that this was once a hotel. This was where Nora Barnacle, the young Galway woman who emigrated to Europe with James Joyce, was working as a chambermaid. Joyce first met Nora on Nassau Street and they walked out for the first time together on 16 June 1904. The entire action of Joyce's novel, *Ulysses*, takes place on 16 June 1904, an indication of the lifelong imprint that day had left on the young writer.

Turn left up Kildare Street from Nassau Street. The building on the corner is the **Heraldic Museum and Genealogical Office(35)**. Look out for the faded but intriguing stone carvings of birds, monkeys playing billiards, even a hare being chased by a dog. Halfway up Kildare Street, on your left, are three important buildings: the **National Library(34)**, **Leinster House (Dáil Eireann)**, and the **National Museum(33)(✔)**. Leinster House faces down Molesworth Street, which is where we go, observing on the left Buswells Hotel, traditional haunt of politicians, and on the right the yellow sandstone Masonic Hall, home of the Grand Lodge of Freemasons in Ireland since 1865. Turn left up Dawson Street. The neo-Gothic **St Ann's Church(37)** is immediately on your left and just beyond, at No. 19, the home of the **Royal Irish Academy**, founded in 1785 to promote the study of the sciences, literature and antiquities. Its first president was the Earl of Charlemont. The building was designed by John Ensor (Merrion Square) in 1769 and has been the home of the RIA since 1852. The library

Buskers on Grafton Street. Photo: Peter Zoeller.

possesses an important collection of Irish manuscripts. Next to the RIA, the **Mansion House(36)** is the home of Dublin's Lord Mayor and is a 1710 building in a Queen Anne style, its original brickwork concealed by Victorian plasterwork. Dublin's most famous Lord Mayor was Alfie Byrne. He occupied the office from 1930 to 1939 and was a very visible figure around town. He is fondly remembered as the waxed-moustached Mayor who carried sweets in his pocket to give out to children on his perambulations.

At the top of Dawson Street cross the road and turn your back to St Stephen's Green. You should now be facing down Dawson Street. On your right, at the far end of the Green, is the imposing, Victorian Shelbourne Hotel, a popular meeting place for the well-heeled and one of Dublin's exclusive hotels. Some of the large houses on your left are long-established, private clubs - Nos 8, 9 and 17. Behind you is **St Stephen's Green(22)**, but a proper visit will take an hour, so perhaps head west to **Grafton Street(19)** where you might stop awhile for a lunchtime snack in one of the many pubs, cafés and restaurants in the area. Grafton Street is Dublin's most fashionable street. **Bewley's Oriental Café**, half-way down the street on the left, was founded by a Quaker family in the early 1840s. Today it is Dublin's most popular café and meeting place. Beside Bewley's is a narrow laneway, Johnston's Court, which connects Grafton Street to the **Powerscourt Townhouse Shopping Centre(20)**. Perhaps this is where you can have lunch, in one of the many small cafés and restaurants in this sensitively restored and cleverly re-developed 18th-century mansion. Before you do, explore the far side of the complex. This is where you will find the original townhouse, with its magnificent drawing-rooms (now upmarket shops and galleries) and exquisite stairway.

The South William Street entrance was the front of the original townhouse, and this is where we exit the building. Opposite is a pedestrian street which leads to the interesting **South City Market** in the

George's Street Arcade. Go right from the Powerscourt Townhouse, to the intersection on whose corners are two important Dublin pubs, the Old Stand and the International Bar (*see A Tour of Dublin's Pubs*). Go down St Andrew Street, passing **St Andrew's Church(18)** on your right, recently converted into Dublin's primary tourist information centre, to where Suffolk Street meets Grafton Street. The long stretch of Nassau Street is in front of you and beside you is the 1988 statue of Molly Malone, the legendary street trader who 'wheeled her wheelbarrow through streets broad and narrow, crying cockles and mussels alive-alive-o'. Turn left. Across the street is **Provost's House**, one of Dublin's finest houses of the period and where the provost of Trinity College has resided since it was built in 1759. The design is believed to be from an original design by Palladio. Three almost identical houses were built around the same time: in Old Burlington Street, London in 1723, in Potsdam in 1755 for Frederick the Great, and the Trinity College Provost's House. This is the only survivor.

Further down the street you will see the curving facade of the **Bank of Ireland(2)** across College Green. From here you get a good idea of the scale of the 1729 Parliament building. **Trinity College(1)(✔)** is to your right, with the figures of Oliver Goldsmith and Edmund Burke facing up Dame Street. Inside the grounds of the College are some exquisite 18th-century buildings, most notably William Chambers Chapel and Examination Hall, Richard Castle's Printing House and Dining Hall (rebuilt), and Thomas Burgh's Library which houses the Book of Kells.

Pass the front gates of the College and cross College Green at the next set of pedestrian lights. The pedestrian island has a statue of the composer Thomas Moore, well known for his 'Moore's Melodies'.

Across the street is the entrance to the **House of Lords(2)(✔)** and a 15 minute detour into this historic chamber is highly recommended. Continue north down Westmoreland Street, past another Bewley's Café and turn right before O'Connell Bridge and walk down Burgh Quay. As you cross the road at the next (Butt) bridge you will leave the clutter of road and railway bridges behind you. From George's Quay you have a magnificent view across the Liffey of the **Custom House(43)**. If it is possible to have a league table of the finest buildings in Dublin, few would not put the Custom House, with its classical elegance, top of the list. To the right of the Custom House is the newly established Financial Services Centre. Cross the next (Matt Talbot) bridge and, keeping the central bus station, Busarus (designed in 1945 by Michael Scott and completed in 1953) on your right, go as far as Gardiner Street, turning into it and walking all the way up to Mountjoy Square. By now you have walked quite a distance, and if you wish to pick up from where you are another day, take a left up Abbey Street, past the **Abbey Theatre(42)**, to O'Connell Street and home.

Trinity College Front Entrance.
Photo: Peter Zoeller.

Gardiner Street is named after Luke Gardiner (1745-98), 18th-century landowner and developer. He was the driving force and the imagination behind the development of key parts of 18th-century northside Dublin, most notably Gardiner's Mall (now O'Connell Street) and Henrietta Street. Gardiner Street was originally 'Old Rope Walk', named after the practice of twisting the fibres as the rope makers walked backwards, in this case up Gardiner Street. At the top of Gardiner Street is **Mountjoy Square(44)**. Building began on the Square in 1792, the west side being the first to be completed. The east side was the last to be completed, and then not until 1818. In its early days the Square was popular among the legal profession.

Leave the Square at the north-west corner and walk left along Gardiner Place. On the right, up towards the top of Temple Street North, is Francis Johnston's classical **St George's Church(46)**. Gardiner Place becomes Great Denmark Street at this point. To the left is **North Great George's Street(47)**, re-emerging in the late 20th century as once again one of the most fashionable streets on the north side of the city. Mid-way down on the left, at No. 35, the **James Joyce Cultural Centre(47)(✔)** is open to the public. Continue to the end of Great Denmark Street and turn left onto **Parnell Square(49)**. O'Connell Street is the wide street in the distance, at the bottom of the hill. Walk down the hill, past the **Gate Theatre(53)** and around the corner to the right, past the **Rotunda Hospital(50)** with Conway's pub's traditional facade across the street. Keeping on the Rotunda side continue around the Square, up to the top where the **Hugh Lane Municipal Gallery of Modern Art(51)(✔)**, the **Dublin Writers Museum(52)(✔)** and the **Garden of Remembrance(49)** will combine to absorb your interest for some time.

Leave the Square by the north-west corner. At the top of Granby Row is the **National Wax Museum(49)**. Turn left into Dorset Street. The first street you pass is Dominick Street, a fashionable street during the 18th century but much of which has long been demolished. Some important buildings remain, notably No. 20, the five-bay Georgian house beyond St Saviour's Church on the left. This was originally the residence of the celebrated builder and stuccodore Robert West. He built the house himself in 1753 and some of the rooms possess the finest plasterwork decoration in Dublin. The mathematician Sir William Rowan Hamilton lived at No. 36, now demolished, while No. 13 was for a time in the 1800s the townhouse of the Dukes of Leinster. The playwright Seán O'Casey lived in

Garden of Remembrance.   Photo: Peter Zoeller.

a flat above St Mary's School for a time. Continue down Dorset Street and turn right up **Henrietta Street(55)**, the earliest Georgian street in Dublin and certainly an impressive one. The houses here are enormous, much larger than most of the Georgian houses you will have seen on this tour. The influential developer, Luke Gardiner, laid out the street, and he lived in No. 10. Go through the passage-way at the top of the street to view the **King's Inns(55)**, a design by James Gandon completed in 1817.

Finish the tour by retracing your footsteps down Henrietta Street and, crossing Bolton Street, turn right and follow the footpath down Capel Street until you see Slattery's pub on your right. Turn left up Mary Street, passing **St Mary's Church(56)** on your right. Ahead of you is the busy pedestrian thoroughfare of Henry Street. Drop into nearby Keating's pub or Bewley's Café for rest and refreshment to finish the day.

Walk Back 1,000 Years -
a walking tour of Medieval Dublin

A walk around Medieval Dublin is a challenge for the imagination, for although there is plenty of documentary evidence to confirm the existence of a bustling community that began to develop over 1,000 years ago, there is little enough to actually see. What there is to see, however, when married to what we *know* existed, provides the interested observer with a fascinating insight into Dublin 1,000 years ago. Places you should visit are indicated with (✔). The numbers in brackets refer to the *Things To See And Do* section and you should consult these entries for more information.

The Tour

We begin the tour standing in the middle of **Father Mathew Bridge**, looking east and downriver towards Dublin Bay (the bridge connects Church Street on the north of the Liffey to Lower Bridge Street on the south). To your left is the splendid 18th-century **Four Courts(60)**, designed by James Gandon and completed in 1802. Three bridges downriver is the pedestrian **Ha'penny Bridge** and beyond that is **O'Connell Bridge**. In AD 841, when the Scandinavian warrior longboats navigated their way up the river below you, the Liffey was around 250 m wide in places. Up the hill to your right was a small agricultural and fishing community and east of this, near where Dublin Castle would be built in 1204, was a monastic settlement. The easily navigated Dublin Bay attracted the Norsemen who had landed in other locations on the east coast of the country, including a brief foray up the Liffey in 837.

Father Mathew Bridge marks the point on the Liffey where the first man-made crossing was constructed. Mounds of stones at regular intervals over which were placed logs and branches provided a sometimes precarious crossing as regular flash floods would frequently sweep all before them. According to the *Annals*, a victorious Ulster army was drowned as it attempted to cross the hurdleford in AD 770. This ancient crossing was called **Áth Cliath** (see page 7). Today, the Gaelic name for Dublin is Baile Átha Cliath (the town of the ford of the hurdles).

Turning right to face south walk up the right side of Bridge Street, passing the **Brazen Head**, Dublin's oldest pub, on your right, and **O'Shea's Merchant**, a celebrated traditional music pub, on your left (see *A Tour of Dublin Pubs*). At the top of the hill turn right and stop at the junction of Cornmarket, St Augustine Street and Thomas Street. This is almost certainly the point where three ancient, long-distance routeways crossed: the Slige Mór which

Four Courts and Father Mathew Bridge.
Photo: Peter Zoeller.

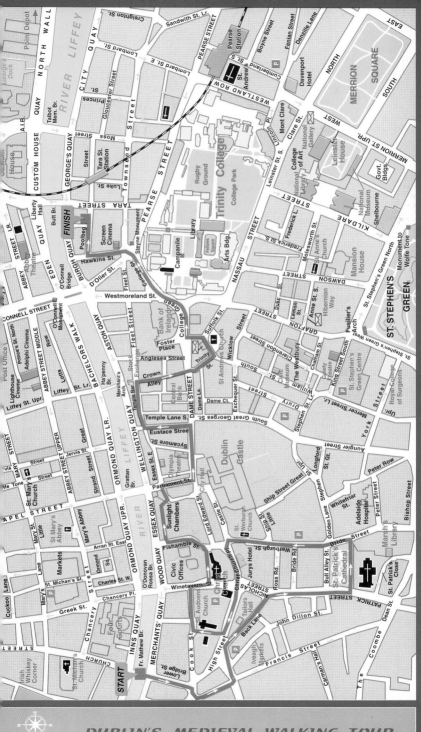

DUBLIN'S MEDIEVAL WALKING TOUR

traversed the country going west; the Slige Midluachra which led to the north, and the Slige Chualann which ran from Tara in County Meath to Glendalough in County Wicklow. The tall and striking church just up Thomas Street is that of Saints Augustine and John (1862-95). It was designed by Edward Welby Pugin and built on the site of the ancient Abbey of St John and a later Augustinian community.

Turn back towards the top of Bridge Street and cross the dual-carriageway on your right to view the lonely piece of stone masonry which stands beside an apartment block. This is part of the old city wall. On the other side of this wall there took place every summer for about two weeks a large fair at which merchants from all over Ireland, and many from abroad, bought and sold every kind of commodity available at that time. This was the Cornmarket. Continue east, going down Back Lane with the 1706 Tailor's Guild Hall on your left. Wolfe Tone and the United Irishmen had their illegal 'Back Lane Parliament' meetings here towards the end of the 18th century. Opposite Tailor's Hall is Mother Redcaps Market and Tavern, formerly the Winstanley Shoe factory and recently restored. The market is open at weekends and is well worth a visit, while the adjoining pub has become a regular live music venue at night. Continue onto Nicholas Street and turn right. The Iveagh Trust Buildings are opposite, down the hill. These were commissioned by the Guinness proprietor at the time, Lord Iveagh, and built between 1901 and 1904. Where Nicholas Street becomes Patrick Street stood St Nicholas's Gate, the most southerly entrance to the medieval town. In front of you is the magnificent **St Patrick's Cathedral(8)(✔)**, founded on possibly the earliest Christian site in Dublin. St Patrick and Jonathan Swift are the two principal names associated with the Cathedral.

Look to your left when you leave the Cathedral. **Marsh's Library(9)(✔)**, Ireland's oldest public library, opened in 1707. Its founder, Archbishop Narcissus Marsh, was an avid collector of rare books and manuscripts and some of these and many other important books, as well as documents and maps, can be viewed. We retrace our steps and enter St Patrick's Park on the other side of the Cathedral. Just inside the gates of the park is a stone marker which confirms that this is the early Christian site of St Patrick's Well. Walk through the park, laid out by Lord Iveagh in 1901. Towards the back you will see an arcade which was

St Patrick's Cathedral.   Photo: Peter Zoeller.

recently restored and now forms a gallery of Irish writers. Exit by the opposite gate to the one through which you entered, turn left and walk along Bride Street. At the traffic lights a memorial to the great classical composer, John Field, reminds us that he was born here in 1782. Field settled in Russia in 1802 and wrote sublime nocturnes in which he anticipated the style and technique of the later Chopin nocturnes. Continue past more of the Iveagh Trust flats on your left and up

Werburgh Street to **St Werburgh's Church(10)** near the top of the street on the right. Not open to the public, you can try calling at the house around the corner where there is a key.

Opposite St Werburgh's Church is a more modern location, that of Leo Burdock's Fish and Chip Shop, renowned throughout Dublin for its generous portions of fried fish and chips. At the top of Werburgh Street you arrive on Christchurch Place. The Lord Edward Fitzgerald pub is on the corner and, across the main road, is the imposing 12th-century **Christ Church Cathedral(6)(✔)**. It is difficult to cross the road at this point, so walk past the Lord Edward to the end of Christchurch Place. The ruins on the corner are of an old church, St Nicholas Within. A number of churches had an appendix after their name, either Within or Without, depending on whether the church was inside or outside the walls of the city. From this corner, looking left and down the hill of Nicholas Street, you can pick out the spire of St Nicholas Without. As you can see, the church you are standing beside did not survive, in fact it had already lost its roof by 1840.

Cross to the Christ Church side. You have the option of visiting **Dublinia(7)(✔)**, situated in the old Synod Hall on the left-hand side of St John's Lane (the entrance fee includes a visit to the Cathedral), or you can go directly to the Cathedral. After your visit turn right outside the Cathedral gates and walk up High Street, and immediately past the Catholic St Audoen's Church descend the stone steps to the church dedicated to the patron saint of the Normandy capital, Rouen, the 12th-century Protestant **St Audoen's Church(11)(✔)**. Continue down St Audoen's Steps and through **St Audoen's Gate** (1240) to Cook Street. The large section of fortified wall which runs along Cook Street is a largely reconstituted version of an original wall built around 1100. At this time the River Liffey was only metres from here at high tide. Cook Street gets its name from the cooks who were obliged to prepare their food outside the highly inflammable city. Turn right and walk past 'Adam and Eve's' Church, named after Adam and Eve's Tavern which occupied this spot, and turn up Winetavern Street. From here you get a good view of the north side of Christ Church Cathedral. To your immediate left are the controversial Civic Offices on Wood Quay, belonging to Dublin Corporation. During excavation work prior to the construction of the buildings, significant archaeological remains of Dublin's earliest Viking settlement were discovered. The artifacts can be viewed in an annexe of the National Museum. These 'bunkers', as they are dismissively called by the majority of Dubliners, designed by a Dublin architect, Sam Stephenson in the early 1980s, were built despite some of the largest street protests the city has seen. The 1994 quayside addition is not attributable to Stephenson.

Turn left up the narrow John's Lane which is just below the Cathedral. This was a medieval street along which once were shops in the recesses of the Cathedral. Arriving on the meandering **Fishamble Street**, in medieval times this was the city market for fish which was openly displayed on the individual traders' stalls. These stalls were called 'shambles', hence the origin of the street's name. Half-way down the street on the right a black plaque at the entrance to the new George Frederic Handel Hotel relates that the old music hall, designed by the celebrated architect Castle in 1741, stood on this site. It was here, on 13 April 1742, that Handel conducted the first ever performance of his *Messiah* to a packed house. In pre-concert publicity ladies were advised not to wear hoops and men were asked not to bring their swords, evidence that a large crowd was expected. Admission was half a guinea and, according to the post-concert notices, the musical event was a huge success. Further down the street the house on the right with the flying buttresses is believed to be the oldest inhabited house in Dublin. Just beyond this house turn right up Exchange Street Lower. On the right is the church of St Michael and John, converted into a Viking Museum, and on the left is the recently excavated Isolde's Tower. Continue on around the corner, following the old line of the city walls, to a short street, Essex Gate. This was the site of Buttevant's Tower in the city wall, demolished in 1675 to create this street. You now reach Parliament Street. To your left is **Grattan Bridge** and the building at the corner on Essex Quay is worth walking down to have a look at. It is the Sunlight Chambers, built around 1900 for a soap manufacturing firm. The history of the manufacture of soap is graphically told in the terracotta carvings on the building. Turn back up towards **City Hall(5)** which faces down Parliament Street. Inside this 18th-century Thomas Cooley building are offices of Dublin Corporation. The City Council meets once a month in a large chamber on the first floor.

Behind City Hall is the courtyard of **Dublin Castle(4)(✔)**. The tour of the Castle includes a guided tour of the State Apartments and the Undercroft Exhibition and is highly recommended. Behind the Castle is a plot of open ground in front of the Coachhouse which is widely believed to be the site of the dark pool formed by the River Poddle (now underground). It is likely that the Vikings kept their ships safe from storms and attack in this sheltered pool they called Dyflinn (Dubh Linn = Black Pool) and there is little doubt that the origin of the name Dublin dates to this place. Viking Dublin was an important slave market and it was from this area that men and women were traded, their destination sometimes as far away as Iceland and Spain.

We finish our tour by walking through **Temple Bar(3)**, an interesting maze of late 16th- and early 17th-century streets. Turn right up Crown Alley and walk along the side of another controversial Sam Stephenson building, the Central Bank, noted for its unusual method of construction in that it was built from the top down, the floors being assembled before being literally hung on the suspending spines. Cross Dame Street and go up Trinity Street on the opposite side, to **St Andrew's Church(18)** now Dublin's primary tourist office. On this corner was

Detail from Sunlight Chambers, Temple Bar. Photo: Peter Zoeller.

situated the Thingmote (Norse Parliament), on a hill which looked down on Hoggen (now College) Green. The name Hoggen probably relates to a series of prehistoric burial mounds in this area.

The last stop on the tour is at the east end of College Street, which runs down the left of Trinity College as you face the front gates. A recently sculpted stone monument was placed in the middle of a miniature city garden to the west of Pearse Street Garda (Police) Station. This is the Steyne, a 13 ft high stone slab which marks the location where the Vikings first landed. The area all around you was submerged by the broad expanse of the Liffey at that time.

Take a well-deserved break in nearby Mulligan's pub on Poolbeg Street.

A Tour of Dublin Pubs

Dublin has never been short of drinking parlours and today is as awash with pubs as it ever has been. This tour is our attempt to get you going in the right direction, to point out some pubs you really shouldn't leave Dublin without seeing. Along the way we have mentioned around 40 pubs. There are, of course, many many more, and because they are not included here is not at all to suggest that these 40 pubs are the only ones worth seeing. No doubt - and we hope you do - you will discover your own favourite pub which is not even featured in this tour. But don't completely ignore our advice. After all, we live here, and we've collectively spent many years in hundreds of Dublin pubs. Those in bold type are the ones we think you should go out of your way to see. Perhaps the best idea is to pop into the odd pub during your daytime meanderings. Many of the city centre pubs are pleasant and certainly different during the daytime. At lunchtime an increasing number of pubs serve hot meals, but every pub will be able to present you with a toasted sandwich and a cup of tea or coffee if it is just a snack you are after. For many pubs, the provision of hot lunches has become an important source of revenue, and some pubs have garnered a reputation more for their food than for the drinking ambience. When evening comes and your meal has been well digested you can embark on the more serious business of viewing pub life in Dublin in its most popular form: crowded bars, noisy with talk, shoulder-to-shoulder drinking. In a sense, what Dublin pubs are all about!

The Tour

We start our tour in the centre of the city, in the *Palace Bar* on Fleet Street, around the corner from Bewley's of Westmoreland Street. This is a very old pub which stands at the entrance to Temple Bar. In the 1940s and 1950s it was a popular haunt for journalists and writers and you can see some interesting memorabilia on the walls recalling those times. The front bar is long and narrow and solid-looking and the best place to have a drink is at the bar. The back of the pub is more like a living-room than a pub. It is always a pleasant place to have a drink because, once seated, you are rarely disturbed. If there are no seats free, patrons will usually not stay in this room but will retreat to the front bar. This means that you are rarely in danger of having a drink accidentally poured over you by a jostled, or jostling, client.

The area around Temple Bar has experienced a spectacular growth in the number of shops and restaurants over the past few years. On the pub front, several new establishments have opened and many of the existing ones have undergone a complete facelift, among them *The Oak* on Dame Street, *The Norseman* on Essex Street, *The Temple Bar* on Temple Bar and the *Oliver St John Gogarty* on Fleet Street. The most interesting pubs are on Parliament Street. *The Front Lounge* is perhaps the coolest and trendiest pub in town. Along the same side is the extravagantly decorated *Turk's Head Chop House*. Across the street is *The Porter House*, which brews its own beers and stout. Finally, on the corner with Dame Street, is the stylish *Thomas Read's*. Continuing west, the *Lord Edward* on Christchurch Place, facing the Cathedral, is named after Lord Edward Fitzgerald, leader of the United Irishmen who was killed in the rebellion of 1798 and is buried in nearby St Werburgh's Church. It can be a nice, quiet place to have a drink. Further west and down near the Liffey on Lower Bridge Street

A TOUR OF DUBLIN PUBS

SCALE 1 : 10 000

0   100   200   300
metres

LIST OF PUBS

1. The Palace Bar
2. The Oak
3. The Crane
4. The Temple Bar
5. Oliver St. John Gogarty
6. The Norseman
7. Bad Bobs
8. Garage Bar
9. The Lord Edward
10. The Brazen Head

11. O'Sheas Merchant
12. Hughes
13. Slattery's
14. Keating's
15. Ryans
16. Conway's
17. The Flowing Tide
18. Mulligan's
19. The Ferryman
20. Kennedy's

21. O'Neill's
22. The Stag's Head
23. The Long Hall
24. Hogan's
25. Neary's
26. McDaid's
27. Kehoe's
28. Davy Byrne's
29. The Bailey
30. The Old Stand

31. The International
32. Cafe En Seine
33. Horseshoe Bar
34. Doheny & Nesbitt
35. O'Donoghue's
36. Toner's
37. An Beal Bocht
38. Slattery's
39. Kitty O'Shea's
40. The Gravedigger
41. Gaffney's

Dublin's Oldest Pub - Brazen Head.
Photo: Peter Zoeller.

are two pubs you really shouldn't miss, the **Brazen Head**, said to be the oldest pub in Ireland, and across the street *O'Shea's Merchant*. The Brazen Head Hotel was established in 1666 on the site of a much older inn, but you'll have to ask the owners about the date of 1198 which is on the sign outside. Leading revolutionaries and nationalists frequented here - Robert Emmet, Wolfe Tone, Daniel O'Connell, Henry Grattan - and some of the leaders of the United Irishmen were arrested here in 1797. O'Shea's Merchant is frequented largely by people from rural Ireland who are living in Dublin or who are in Dublin for a day or two. It is crowded every night and the live traditional music can sometimes be superb.

There is a small wooden part of the floor at the end of the bar where traditional Irish set dancing is enjoyed on an impromptu basis. Across the Liffey, behind the Four Courts, is another pub with a reputation for traditional music and sets (set dancing). This is **Hughes** on Chancery Street. It is a much quieter pub and a pleasant place to have a drink and enjoy the music. Another pub, not far from here, which has a nightly session of traditional music, is **Slattery's** on Capel Street, and up the nearby Abbey Street is a cleverly restored pub, **Keating's.** The pub has established a reputation for excellent live traditional music. Staying on the north side, walk the length of the quays, upriver, to **Ryan's of Parkgate Street**. This section of the Liffey Quays can be a lonely enough place to find yourself in at night-time, so if you are travelling alone perhaps come back later on your way out to the Phoenix Park (see page 62). Ryan's is one of Dublin's finest pubs, and well worth the walk. It has four snugs (small compartments with a latched door so you won't be disturbed by those in the main bar) and a beautifully ornate interior. The Scotch granite frontage is particularly handsome. This is a well-run establishment, always glisteningly clean and serving excellent pints. You are now a long walk from O'Connell Street, so perhaps you should take a bus or a taxi back into the city centre, to our next pub which is opposite the Rotunda Maternity Hospital on Parnell Street. **Conway's** has a lovely traditional frontage, though its interior, while handsome, can sometimes look a bit scruffy. The oval-shaped mahogany bar has propped up many an expectant father whose better half was doing the difficult job across the street.

There are no pubs of note on O'Connell Street, but a brief diversion upriver along Bachelor's Walk will bring us to two pubs which reflect

Mulligan's Pub, Poolbeg Street. Photo: Peter Zoeller.

the changing times in Dublin's pub culture. *Zanzibar* is new, large and brash and can hold about fifteen hundred revellers at the one time: a remarkable fact is that it manages to do just that on several nights every week. It fronts onto the river. *Pravda* is more stylish, more self-conscious and equally successful. It can be found opposite the Ha'penny Bridge, at the entrance to Liffey Street, beside the 'Hags with the Bags' statue.

At the other side of O'Connell Street, along Abbey Street Lower and diagonally across from the Abbey Theatre is the *Flowing Tide,* always full of actors, both those who make a living out of it and those who practise their amateur art, leaning against the bars of Dublin pubs, issuing their own impassioned and sometimes inebriated soliloquys to any soul who will listen. The wood-panelled interior is covered in posters from the Abbey and Peacock theatres and these are a fascinating record of some of the great plays and performances seen across the road over the years. Be sure to place your glass on the table before you try to read the posters on the ceiling! Directly across the Liffey from here, on Poolbeg Street, is *Mulligan's,* one of Dublin's most famous pubs, long believed to serve the best pint of Guinness in the city. In truth, many pubs can serve just as good a pint but in the old days Mulligan's creamy pint was the classic pint. This is a rough and ready pub, always busy, generally noisy, and possessing one of Dublin's finest pub frontages.

The next pub we visit is *O'Neill's* on Suffolk Street, with five separate bars, one a glass-panelled cocktail bar. Very popular with Trinity College students, this is one of the busiest, and noisiest, pubs in town. Its corner facade is striking and you can enter and leave by Trinity Street or Suffolk Street. The pub is built on or very near the site of the Viking Thingmote (Parliament). Dame Lane, a straight, narrow street off Trinity Street, boasts one of Dublin's most attractive bars, the *Stag's Head,* with its original stained-glass windows and a magnificent mahogany bar. The pub specialises in pub lunches. Up nearby South Great George's Street is an even more attractive pub, the *Long Hall.* Built in the 1880s, the pub has a unique interior, with a variety of crystal chandeliers, a beautifully decorated bar with antique glass and a fine pendulum clock. The bartending here is the perfect blend of professionalism and friendliness. Across the street is a newly renovated pub and an overnight success, *Hogan's.* Classily done in black with large windows and a sparse feel to the interior, this pub attracts a young, trendy clientele.

Heading across towards Grafton Street, *Neary's* on Chatham Street is a popular haunt of actors from the Gaiety Theatre on parallel South King Street. The fine stone frontage is complemented by the plush atmosphere inside, with marble-topped bar, mahogany surrounds and brass lighting. Nearby, on Harry Street, is *McDaid's,* famous for the patronage it received in the 1950s by three Irish writers, Brendan Behan, Brian O'Nolan (Flann O'Brien) and Patrick Kavanagh. The pub has been renovated and it has lost much of its, admittedly shabby, past character. Nevertheless, it is always a busy, lively place and is an essential visit for the Behan, O'Brien and Kavanagh fans. Across Grafton Street from McDaid's is South Anne Street, and here is a real, old-style pub, with its snugs, low lighting and cluttered atmosphere. You won't get live music in *Kehoe's* but you'll get plenty of conversation.

On parallel Duke Street is a famous pub with Joyce connections. *Davy Byrne's* is celebrated in *Ulysses* in a scene which describes the novel's hero, Bloom, taking his lunch here. On Bloomsday every June this pub plays a central part in the day's celebrations (*see Calendar of Events*). The pub has undergone many interior transformations and would today be unrecognisable to Joyce. Opposite Davy Byrne's is *The Bailey*, another pub with long, literary traditions, though the pub we see today bears little resemblance to the literary meeting place of forty years ago. Across Grafton Street and onto Wicklow Street we find two pubs on opposite corners, the *Old Stand* and the *International Bar.* The Old Stand has traditionally been a meeting place for rugby followers before an international game and it is a comfortable city-centre bar and lounge to relax in after a long day's touring. The International Bar is much more traditional in character and hasn't changed at all over the years. Its heavy mahogany counter, high ceiling, ornate glass windows and passing-through clientele combine to make this one of Dublin's more interesting places to have a drink.

Photo: Peter Zoeller.

Opposite the Mansion House on Dawson Street is a trendy, upmarket pub, *Café en Seine*. The extravagantly long bar and very high ceiling create a terrific feeling of space when you walk in. Unfortunately, this is just an illusion because the bar is too narrow for the number of patrons who regularly crowd this place out. Even going to the toilet becomes an ordeal. The best time by far to view this magnificently lavish creation is in the morning when you can have a coffee and brioche and sit and wonder if this is really Dublin, or did you get the wrong flight and end up in Brussels. Around the corner you can continue your observations of the well-heeled, trendy set in the ***Horseshoe Bar*** of the Shelbourne Hotel. The hotel has long been a magnet for the jet set and for those who like to watch them. The legal profession is above all of this: they form one of the core groups which regularly inhabit this illustrious bar.

A little further down the street, on Merrion Row, is another pub which attracts members of the legal profession, as well as media people and politicians from nearby Leinster House. This is ***Doheny & Nesbitt's,*** a no-nonsense, old-style traditional pub, with a heavy mahogany counter, wooden partitions which create semi-private drinking stalls, and a fine display of drinks behind the counter. Across the street, towards the Shelbourne, is Dublin's most famous music pub, ***O'Donoghue's.*** This is where the legendary ballad group, The Dubliners, started off. Although these days it has become a veritable tourist trap, it still remains an essential place to visit, if only to see just how many people can actually fit into a small Dublin pub if the will is there. Just beyond Doheny & Nesbitt's on the other side of the street is ***Toner's,*** a fine Victorian pub with a characteristic snug. The pub seems old and worn yet solidly resisting any temptation to follow the path of modernisation which many pubs have taken. Modernisation of Dublin pubs frequently results in pastiche, an irretrievable loss of character and ironically a big upturn in business, essentially because more and more people these days are looking for a pub which will provide them with semi-plush seating in comfortable surroundings. Toner's is in the old vein of Dublin pubs, as far removed from the ethos of modernisation as one could possibly imagine.

Finally, some pubs worth going out of the way to see. At the top of Rathmines Road, ***Slattery's*** has a beautiful Victorian frontage and a variety of bars, all in a traditional style. Note the snug and the low counter in the front section. On the northside of the city, the ***'Gravediggers'*** in Glasnevin should not be missed. The name on the outside is ***John Kavanagh*** - for this pub belongs to a Dublin family of that name - but the name 'Gravediggers' comes from the fact that it is situated at the old entrance to Prospect (Glasnevin) Cemetery (see page 65). It has a long and interesting history and its proprietor Eugene Kavanagh proudly carries on a six-generation family

Doheny & Nesbitt's Pub, Baggot Street. Photo: Peter Zoeller.

tradition in this old, rambling and full-of-character public house. Last but far from least is ***Gaffney's*** at 5/6 Fairview Road. This is a finely preserved Victorian pub. Its unusual and striking frontage sets the scene for a remarkable interior, clean as a whistle, totally genuine, and very friendly bar staff and patrons. After your brisk walk along the seafront in the bracing wind, what better place to relax than in a pub which combines the best traditions of Dublin pubs.

Day And Half-Day Excursions Outside Dublin City

There are many places of exceptional interest and beauty within one hour's drive from Dublin city. The five tours in this section are popular touring areas and you will be able to find regular bus-and-guide excursions from the city centre. See the Tours section in *Getting To And Around Dublin*. If you are in Dublin for only a couple of days but want to get out of the city for one of those days, a trip to the scenic Wicklow Mountains with a visit to the monastic site of Glendalough is certainly the most picturesque.

Excursion A

Dun Laoghaire - Sandycove - Dalkey - Bray

Dun Laoghaire (pronounced *dun leary*) was called Kingstown from 1821 - when King George IV sailed from here following a visit to Ireland - until 1922, when Ireland became an independent free state. It was to here that the first train in Ireland travelled in 1834 from Westland Row. A regular ferry service to Holyhead in Wales has operated out of here for almost one hundred and fifty years. The town is a seaside suburb of Dublin and is busy at all times, however it is the magnificent harbour, built between 1817 and 1842, that is the main feature of the town. The two piers enclose some one hundred hectares of protected harbour. The East Pier is 1,290 m long, the West Pier 1,548 m, each pier ending in a lighthouse. With the sweep of Dublin Bay before you, a walk along one of the piers in fine weather is a treat.

The **National Maritime Museum** has an interesting collection of sea-related exhibits. Of particular interest is the French ship's longboat captured in Bantry Bay in 1796, but this is just one of many unusual items on display. *Opening Hours:* May-Sept: Tues-Sun 13.00-17.00. Sun only in Oct. Open for short periods during Christmas and Easter. Admission: Adults £1.50, Senior Citizens/Children 80p, Family £5. *Tel: (01) 2800969.*

You can easily walk the 1 km to **Sandycove** along the seafront. Sandycove village, away from the seafront, is small and largely unspoilt and has some interesting little boutiques, a fine delicatessen, a few cafés and two popular pubs, the *Eagle House* and *Fitzgerald's*. Down at the sea is the Forty-Foot, a popular bathing spot which for a long time and

Dun Laoghaire Harbour.   Photo: Peter Zoeller.

until relatively recently was off bounds to women bathers. Nearby is the **James Joyce Museum,** housed in one of the Martello Towers which were built around the Irish coast between 1804 and 1815 to help defend the country from a Napoleonic invasion which never happened. This tower is the scene of the opening of Joyce's novel *Ulysses* and the museum's collection includes two death masks of Joyce, various letters, photographs and documents, and a number of editions of Joyce's work. _Opening Hours:_ April-Oct Mon-Sat 10.00-13.00 and 14.00-17.00. Sun 14.00-18.00. Open every Tues outside the high season. For all other times contact the Museum at *(01) 2809265* or the Dublin Writers Museum, *(01) 6057700.* Admission: Adults £2.60, Senior Citizens/Students £2.10, Children £1.30.

South of Sandycove is the attractive town of **Dalkey**, full of small shops, restaurants, cafés, and a generous quota of pubs, of which *Queens* and *The Club* are the best known. George Bernard Shaw spent many youthful summers at Torca Cottage on Dalkey Hill, and later the town was immortalised in Flann O'Brien's novel *The Dalkey Archive* and more recently in Hugh Leonard's evocative play, *Da*. The narrow roads around the town are full of interesting and quite exclusive residences. The Vico Road south of the town affords a wonderful view of the southern sweep of Dublin Bay. This part of the Dublin coast has

Coliemore Harbour and Dalkey Island.
Photo: Peter Zoeller.

been likened, on hot sunny days, to the Bay of Naples. In the summer you can hire a boat to take you to Dalkey Island, rich in birdlife and possessing its very own Martello Tower. Killiney Hill, further south, offers splendid views of the bay and the Dublin and Wicklow Mountains.

The Victorian seaside resort of **Bray** is only worth a visit if you have time to walk some of the Cliff Walk between Bray and Greystones. The town was once a fashionable resort for Dublin holidaymakers but the picturesque seafront with its lovely promenade has suffered from neglect over the years. One of the houses belonging to the terrace which looks down the promenade from the north end was the home of James Joyce between 1889 and 1891. Behind this terrace, the Harbour Bar is an interesting place to have a drink, full of all kinds of odds and ends relating to life on the ocean waves. With the

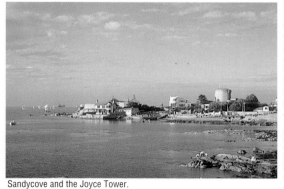

Sandycove and the Joyce Tower.
Photo: Peter Zoeller.

introduction of the rapid rail, DART, in the late 1980s, Bray's population has increased quite dramatically and the town has lost much of its character as a result.

All these towns can be reached on the DART which runs regularly between Bray and Howth.

Excursion B

Powerscourt - Glendalough - Russborough House

Head for Enniskerry, the estate village of Powerscourt House. The village existed because of the nearby estate, but today it survives independently, a compact little village nestled among surrounding hills. A little further on is **Powerscourt House and Gardens**. The house was designed by the noted architect Richard Castle in 1740 for the powerful 18th-century Powerscourt family. Castle was responsible for some of the finest Georgian town and country houses in Dublin, Wicklow and Kildare. The entire Powerscourt estate covers an area of approximately 14,000 acres. In 1974, on the eve of a party to celebrate the restoration of the house, a fire swept through the building, leaving a burnt out shell where several hours earlier had stood a magnificent period mansion. Another major restoration job allowed the building to be opened to the public in 1997, and the house and gardens are now one of the most visited sites in the entire country. The Gardens were laid out during the 19th century and are well worth seeing. A 6 km signposted walk will lead you to **Powerscourt Waterfall**, the highest in Ireland and Britain at 120 m, but you can also drive there along one of the roads outside the estate.

House and Gardens Opening Hours:
Daily. Mar-Oct 09.30-17.30. Nov-Feb 09.30-dusk (Gardens), 09.30-17.30 (House). Admission: Combined House and Gardens: Adults £5, Senior Citizens/Students £4.50, Children £3. House only: £1.50, £1.30, £1. Gardens only: £3.50, £3.20, £2. Waterfall: Summer 09.30-19.00. Winter 10.30-dusk. Admission: £2, £1.50, £1.
Tel: (01) 2046000

There is a fine café and restaurant in the house, open all year round.

Glendalough (*Gleann Dá Locha* in Gaelic meaning *Valley of the Two Lakes*) is a ruined monastic settlement, founded in the 6th century by the hermetic saint, Kevin. Situated in magnificent mountain and valley scenery, it was an important centre of learning for many centuries and survived Viking plundering in the 9th and 10th centuries and Anglo-Norman invasion in the 14th century, until its final demise after the Reformation in the 16th century. Today, the site contains a perfectly preserved round tower, cathedral ruins, a 12th-century Priest's House and St Kevin's Church, also called St Kevin's Kitchen on account of the tower's likeness to a chimney. There is also a fine high

Powerscourt House and Gardens, County Wicklow. Photo: Peter Zoeller.

cross and many graves of some antiquity. There is a very good interpretative centre beside the ruined monastery in which you can watch an audio-visual presentation on Ireland's monastic settlements with particular

Glendalough, County Wicklow.
Photo: Peter Zoeller.

emphasis, naturally enough, on
Glendalough. There is also an
interesting exhibition which includes a
model of the monastery at the height
of its influence. Outside the busy
tourist season, when the site can
sometimes be overflowing with
visitors, there is an atmosphere of
peace and tranquillity. Throughout the
year you can find that same
tranquillity if you walk away from the
site and along the lakes into the heart
of the valley.

Interpretative Centre Opening Hours:
Daily. Jun-Aug 09.00-18.30. Sept-
mid-Oct 09.30-18.00. Mid-Oct-mid-
Mar 09.30-17.00. Mid-Mar-31 May
09.30-18.00. Last entry forty-five
minutes before closing. Admission,
which in high season always includes
a guided tour: Adults £2, Senior
Citizens/Groups £1.50,
Students/Children £1, Family £5.
Tel: (0404) 45352/45325. Entry to the
monastic site is free.

You can drive to **Russborough
House** from Glendalough, taking the
road to Blessington across the
mountains. This is a wonderfully
scenic drive, so take your time. At
Blessington turn left and look for the

signs for Russborough House a few
kilometres out the road on your right.
The house was designed by Richard
Castle, who also designed
Powerscourt House, and it was
completed in 1750. The house was
one of the most splendid Georgian
classical mansions in Ireland when it
was built, its style influencing many
other later country houses on the east
coast of the country. The celebrated
stuccodores, the Francini brothers
from Switzerland, were responsible
for much of the superb plasterwork in
the principal rooms. The house was
bought by Sir Alfred Beit in 1952 and
he and his wife continued to expand
the spectacular collection of paintings
his uncle, Alfred Beit, had amassed.
The Beit Art Collection is the main
reason people visit Russborough
House. The collection contains
important works by Goya, Vermeer,
Rubens, Velazquez, Gainsborough
and Murillo, although some of the
'jewels in the crown' were stolen in an
infamous robbery in 1986.

Opening Hours: April/May: Sun/
Holidays 10.30-17.30. June/July/Aug:
seven days a week 10.30-17.30. Sept:
Mon-Sat 10.30-14.30. Sun/Holidays
10.30-17.30. Oct: Sun/Holidays
10.30-17.30. Admission: Adults £3,
Students £2, Children £1. *Tel: (045)
865239 (seasonal).* The route back to
Dublin is through Blessington and is a
straight run of around 30 km.

Excursion C

**Howth - Malahide Castle -
Newbridge House - Skerries
– Ardgillan Castle
– National Ecology Centre**

The northern sweep of Dublin Bay is
brought to a hilly end by **Howth
Head** (the name Howth is a derivative
of the Norse *hoved* meaning *head*).
Howth village is situated on the
northern side of the peninsula, where
the harbour creates an idyllic setting
(the DART train from Dublin stops
almost at the harbour). It was at this
harbour that King George IV landed
in 1821 and you can see an imprint of
his footstep where he disembarked on
the west pier. Howth is a popular

sailing centre with the newly-built marina offering the most modern of facilities. Property prices on Howth Head are among the highest in Dublin and some of the most scenic parts of the headland vie for exclusivity with Dalkey and Killiney at the southern end of the bay. There is a lovely walk you can take from the harbour which will bring you around the unspoilt eastern side of the Head, and if you go far enough you will be rewarded with a fine view across Dublin Bay. *Howth Castle* (partly ruined and not open to the public) *and Gardens* are worth seeing, as is the *National Transport Museum* which is situated in the Castle grounds and has many interesting exhibits, including some of the original Dublin trams which were de-commissioned in 1959.

Transport Museum Opening Hours: Open all year round at weekends 14.00-17.00. Open June/July/Aug on Mon-Fri 10.00-18.00. Admission: Adults £1.50, Children 50p.
Tel: (01) 8480831.
Further up the coast is the attractive village of Malahide, with colourful shopfronts, a variety of restaurants, lively pubs and the impressive **Malahide Castle** just outside the town. The Norman Talbot de Malahide family lived in the Castle from 1185 to 1976. Now open to the public, the tour is a veritable journey through the architectural development of the Castle over its lifespan, from the original defensive tower to what was to become eventually a country mansion. Some fine paintings from the National Portrait Collection are here, and the period furniture adds to the overall effect. The Castle is a popular

attraction for both Irish and overseas tourists throughout the year. For model train fanatics the *Fry Model Railway Museum* in the gardens of the Castle is a rare and unique collection of handmade models of Irish trains from the introduction of rail to the modern-day period.

Opening Hours: Castle: Apr-Oct Mon-Sat 10.00-17.00. Sun/Hols 11.00-18.00. Nov-Mar: Mon-Fri 10.00-17.00. Sat/Sun/Hols 14.00-17.00. Closed for tours 12.45-14.00, though restaurant remains open. Admission: Adults £3.10, Senior Citizens/Students £2.60, Children £1.70, Family £8.50. *Tel: (01) 8462184.* Restaurant and Craft Shop.

Opening Hours: Railway Museum – Apr-Sept: Mon-Fri 10.00-18.00. Sat 10.00-17.00. Sun/Hols 14.00-18.00. Closed Fri during Apr & May. Oct-Mar: Sat/Sun/Hols 14.00-17.00. Closed for tours 13.00-14.00. Admission: Adults £2.85, Senior Citizens/Students £2.15, Children

Howth Village and Harbour.   Photo: Peter Zoeller.

£1.65. Family £7.75.
Tel: (01) 8463779
Combined ticket to Castle and Museum: Adults £4.75, Senior Citizens/Students £3.70, Children £2.70, Family £12.25.
Newbridge House (1736-43) is a little north of Malahide, at Donabate.The house, set on three hundred and fifty acres of parkland,

was built to a design by Richard Castle and contains elaborate stucco plasterwork by Robert West. There is a fully restored courtyard, surrounded by a dairy, estate worker's house, carpenter's shop and a blacksmith forge.

Opening Hours: April-Sept: Tues-Sat 10.00-17.00; Sun/Holidays 14.00-18.00. Oct-Mar: Weekends and holidays only 14.00-17.00. Admission to House: Adults £2.95, Senior Citizens/Students £2.55, Children £1.60, Family £7.95.

There is a traditional farm attached to the house which you can visit.
Tel: (01) 8436534

The seaside town of **Skerries** is well worth driving the 10 km from Donabate to see. It is a quiet town with a small pier and some fine windswept walks, like the coastal one to Loughshinny. St Patrick is believed to have landed in Ireland at this point on the eastern coast, although other theories suggest he landed much further south, down towards Wexford. There is a thriving sailing community in Skerries, and one gets the impression that, despite the town's proximity to Dublin, it could well be on the west coast of the country such is the sense of independence from the capital the town exudes. Further north along the coast, towards Balbriggan, **Ardgillan Castle** is set among one-hundred-and-ninety-four acres of

rolling pasture land, mixed woodland and gardens. The Castle was built in 1738 and is furnished in Georgian/Victorian style.

Opening Hours: Apr-Sept: Tues-Sun/Hols 11.00-18.00 (open daily in Jul/Aug). Oct-Mar: Tues-Sun & Hols 11.00-16.30. The park is open daily 10.00-dusk. Admission: Free to Castle and grounds. Guided tour: Adults £2.75, Senior Citizens /Students £1.75 Family £6.50.

Tel: (01) 8492212

Five miles south-east of Drogheda, near the little village of Laytown, is the **National Ecology Centre,** based in a renovated 18th-century farm complex set in extensive grounds. Its facilities include a two acre walled organic garden, an energy courtyard with a variety of alternative energy exhibits of wind, water and solar power, an ecoshop with a range of environmentally friendly goods and an organic winery which produces wine from the centre's own produce.

Tel: (041) 27572 for details of opening hours.

Excursion D

The Boyne Valley Tour

You will need to devote a full day to this most intriguing and historic of tours. We begin our tour by taking the

Newgrange.   Photo: Peter Zoeller.

N2 to the village of **Slane**, built on a hill overlooking the **River Boyne**. North of the village is the Hill of Slane where St Patrick lit a fire at Easter AD 433, thus beginning his evangelisation of Ireland. A fire destroyed much of the fine interior of Lord Henry Mountcharles' nearby Slane Castle in 1992. Over the past ten years the grounds of the Castle have been the venue for some of the world's biggest rock and pop stars, among them Bob Dylan, the Rolling Stones, Bruce Springsteen, David Bowie, U2 and The Verve.

Follow the signpost to **Brú na Bóinne Visitor Centre,** east of the town. The Centre is designed to present the archaeological heritage of the Boyne Valley which includes the megalithic passage tombs of Newgrange and Knowth. All visitors wishing to visit Newgrange and Knowth must go through the Visitor Centre.

Newgrange dates to 3,000BC. The 75 m diameter, 13 m high circular tumulus is made up of 180,000 tons of black and white stones, largely covered with earth and grass. The entrance leads, by a narrow 20 m passage lined with massive slabs of stone, to an interior chamber decorated with geometric and spiral drawings. During the Winter Solstice, when the sun reaches a precise height in the sky, its rays pierce a narrow opening in the tumulus and, through a tiny passage to the interior of the construction, illuminate the burial chamber inside. Newgrange is part of the three principal centres of Brú na Bóinne (Palace of the Boyne) that includes nearby **Dowth** and **Knowth**.

Newgrange Opening Hours:
June/Mar/Apr: daily 09.30-17.30. May: daily 09.00-18.30. Jun-mid-Sept: daily 09.00-19.00. Mid-Sept-end-Sept: daily 09.00-18.30. Oct: daily 09.30-17.30. Admission: Interpretative Centre only: Adult £2, Senior Citizens/Group rate £1.50, Children/Students £1, Family £5. Newgrange itself: £3, £2, £1.25, £7.50. Knowth: same as Interpretative Centre. Combined ticket to all three: £5, £3.50, £2.25, £12.50. Last tour of monuments 1¹/₂ hours before closing time of the Visitor Centre. This is an extremely busy place during the

Monasterboice. Photo: Peter Zoeller.

summer, so arrive early to avoid disappointment.
Tel: (041) 24488

Not far from Newgrange is an obelisk marking the site of the historic **Battle of the Boyne** in 1690 in which the forces of Protestant King William of Orange came face to face with and overcame the forces of Catholic James II. Ulster Protestants commemorate this famous victory on 12 July every year in marches throughout the Province of Ulster. Drive along the banks of the Boyne to **Drogheda** for lunch. The Vikings established a settlement here in AD 911. Later, the Normans constructed a heavily fortified town which by the 14th century was one of Ireland's most important towns. In 1649 Oliver Cromwell attacked the town, killing some three thousand of the garrison and its inhabitants in a typical Cromwellian bloodbath. Sections of the old town ramparts have survived, the best example being St Lawrence's Gate. The church of St Peter (1791) contains the head of St Oliver Plunkett, former Bishop of Armagh who was martyred in Tyburn in 1681 and canonised in 1975. Across the river is Millmount where the 14th-century Magdalene Tower dominates the surrounding area. This was part of a Dominican friary founded in 1224.

Leave Drogheda by the T1 and head for the ruins of **Mellifont Abbey**, founded by the Cistercian monk St Malachy in 1142. The partially restored cloister dates from around 1200. Among the most interesting ruins to see are the 10 m diameter octagonal lavabo where the monks washed their hands, a square tower, and a large church. (*Telephone Visitor Centre: (041) 9826459*). Leaving Mellifont head for Collon and turn right for **Monasterboice**, a monastic settlement founded by St Buithe in the 5th century. The ruins of the monastic enclosure contain a cemetery, two 13th-century church ruins, a partly destroyed round tower and the magnificent high cross of Muiredach (10th-century) and two later high crosses of which the West Cross is the more important. Muiredach's Cross, in particular, is a fine example of celtic art stone carving.

Head back to Slane and continue through the crossroads in the direction of Navan, county town of Meath. The ruined Dunmoe Castle dates from the late 15th century, while nearby a Romanesque doorway and crucifix has been added to the Donaghmore

Mellifont Abbey.   Photo: Peter Zoeller.

round tower. Continue towards Trim, a quiet country town, dominated by the ruins of King John's Castle, built by Hugh de Lacy in 1173 and enlarged and fortified in the 13th century to become the largest Anglo-Norman citadel in Ireland, when it was seized by King John. The other castle in Trim, Talbot Castle, was built in 1415 by Sir John Talbot, Lord

Lieutenant of Ireland, on the site of a 12th-century Augustinian abbey, St Mary's. Both Jonathan Swift and the Duke of Wellington have associations nearby: Swift was curate in Laracor and the Duke of Wellington is claimed by some and disputed by others to have been born in nearby Dangan Castle. Those who dispute the Duke's birthplace conform to the generally held view that he was born on Merrion Street in Dublin. The Hill of Tara is close by. This was the ancient capital of the Celtic High Kings of Ireland and an important centre of paganism until the coming of Christianity and St Patrick's visit to the court of King Laogaire. A newly-built Visitor Centre provides an audio-visual show and guided tours of the site.

Opening Hours: May-Mid-June: daily 10.00-17.00. Mid-June-mid-Sept: daily 09.30-18.30. Mid-Sept-end-Oct: daily 10.00-17.00. Admission: Adult £1.50, Senior Citizens/Group rate £1, Children/Students 60p, Family £4. *Tel: (046) 25903*
Continue south along the N3 to Dublin.

Excursion E

Kildare - National Stud - Japanese Gardens - Castletown House

County Kildare possesses the most fertile land in Ireland. Because of this, the county has always been associated with large farmland estates and some of the most magnificent of all the 18th-century stately mansions were built in this county. It is also an area noted for the international success of its horse breeding industry, and for Ireland's most famous racecourse, the Curragh. The tour can be done in half a day, however if you include a visit to the Georgian mansion, Castletown House, you will need the whole day. Take the unappealing motorway route along the N7, bypassing the small towns of Naas and Newbridge and on to the Curragh Plain, with the largely concealed Irish Army barracks on the left and the Curragh Racecourse on the right. This is where thousands of punters, many glamorously attired,

flock to see the Irish Derby every June. Continue to **Kildare**, the name of which is derived from the Irish *Cill Dara* meaning *Church of the Oak*. St Brigid founded a monastery here in the 5th century. The Cathedral of St Brigid was begun in 1229 but was almost completely destroyed in the 16th century. The Victorian reconstruction was completed in 1875 and now serves the Protestant community around Kildare. The round tower dates to the 12th century. Outside the town is the **National Stud**, a State-run bloodstock farm since 1943. There are guided tours of the stables and interesting stories about some of the famous horses which passed through here. A skeletal *Arkle* stands to remind us that here was one of the greatest and certainly most loved Irish horses of all time. Beside the National Stud are the intriguing **Japanese Gardens**, well worth a visit even if flowers and plants are not your particular speciality. The Gardens were laid out in 1906 by a Japanese gardener named Eito and they represent the seven ages of man (and, presumably, woman). A new feature of the site is the commemorative Garden of St Fiacra, laid out for the Millennium within a natural setting of woodland, wetland, lakes and islands. *Opening Hours:* 12 Feb-12 Nov: daily 09.30-last admission 17.00. Combined entrance to National Stud, Japanese Gardens and Garden of St Fiacra: Adults £6, Senior Citizens/Students £4.50, Children £3, Family £14. *Tel: (045) 521617/522963.* Advance booking essential.
On your way back to Dublin go by Maynooth, ancient seat of the Earls of Kildare whose enormous castle (now ruined) once dominated the town. (The present Parliament House in Kildare Street in Dublin was built for the Duke of Leinster, Earl of Kildare in 1745-8 and is still known as *Leinster House* - see page 49.) Today

County Kildare, renowned for its horse breeding.
Photo: Bord Fáilte.

the town is an established university town and is the home of the most important Catholic seminary in Ireland, St Patrick's College. South-east of Maynooth is the attractive but sprawling manor village of Celbridge. Jonathan Swift often came here to visit his companion, Esther 'Vanessa' Vanhomrigh and there is a seat by the river where they often sat. North-east of the village is the early Georgian stately mansion, **Castletown House** (1722). This was the largest private house in Ireland, designed by Alessandro Galilei for the Speaker of the Irish House of Commons, William Conolly, with the entrance hall, colonnade and wings probably carried out by Edward Lovett Pearce, architect of the old Parliament House on College Green in Dublin. Stucco work on the stairway is accredited to the celebrated Francini brothers. An interesting feature in the estate grounds is the curious looking Conolly's Folly, believed to have been designed by Richard Castle in 1740. *Opening Hours:* Check with the tourist office in Dublin *(01-6024000)* or Kildare *(045-522696, seasonal office)* as the opening times given here may vary. Apr-Sept: Mon-Fri 10.00-18.00. Sat 11.00-18.00. Sun 14.00-18.00. Oct: Mon-Fri 10.00-17.00. Sun/Holidays 14.00-17.00. Nov-Mar: Sun/Holidays 14.00-17.00. Admission: Adults £2.50, Senior Citizens £1.75, Students/Children £1. Castletown House is about 21 km from Dublin.

DIRECTORY

Places To Stay In Dublin

Apart from the rush on beds during July and August, you will generally not experience too much difficulty in finding a suitable place to rest your weary head in Dublin after a day's travel or touring. The number of hotels, guesthouses, bed & breakfasts (B&B) and hostels is increasing every year to keep up with the enormous demand. That doesn't mean you should be complacent, for it is always a good idea to book in advance no matter what time of the year you are travelling. If you haven't booked in advance you can save yourself a lot of trouble by telephoning the Tourist Office Reservation Number 1800 668668 and they will make your reservation for you for a fee of £3, payable by credit card only. A comprehensive accommodation guide, Dublin *Accommodation Guide*, is available on request from your nearest Irish Tourist Board office.

As in all cities, prices will vary considerably between the low season and the high season. The price indications we give here are to be taken as indications only. The grading of accommodation has recently been given to independent agencies. Hotels are star graded 1-5, and guesthouses graded 1-4. A small number of hotels are graded U (unclassified), N (too new to be classified) or R (refurbishment recently completed). Prices vary considerably, depending on where you are. For example, a typical three-star hotel in Dublin will cost between £50 and £80 per person per night, whereas in Donegal the rates will be between £25 and £50. An average B&B will cost between £20 and £40 per person, but some of the plusher ones in the fashionable districts of Dublin can cost up to £50 per person per night. A dormitory bed in a hostel will cost around £13 per night. Some hostels provide single, double and family room accommodation at quite competitive prices. Standards vary, but they are all clean and well run.

Naturally, the closer you are to the city centre the more you are likely to pay. An exception to this rule are the numerous hotels and guesthouses in the southern suburb of Ballsbridge. Some of the best and most exclusive hotels in the city are in this leafy, Victorian district.

The most exclusive hotels are generally regarded as the **Shelbourne**, **Conrad**, **Westbury**, **Clarence** and **Gresham**, all in the city centre, and the **Berkeley Court**, **Burlington** and **Jurys Towers** which are located in the fashionable Ballsbridge district, a couple of kilometres south of the city centre. Contenders for inclusion in this elite list are the refurbished **Mont Clare** and the **Davenport** and the new **Merrion**, all a stone's throw from the National Gallery on Merrion Square, and the **Hibernian** in Ballsbridge. A list of many of the hotels in the city and suburbs is provided below, together with a selected list of guesthouses and some hostels. As the building of new hotels and other types of accommodation is increasing at an incredible rate in the city, this list does not pretend to be exhaustive. A complete list of Bord Fáilte approved accommodation can be purchased from any Bord Fáilte office, cost £5.

South City Hotels (within 3 km of O'Connell Street)

Adams Trinity, Dame Street, D2 ☎01 6707100 N
Berkeley Court Hotel, Ballsbridge, D4 ☎01 6601711 *****
Bewley's Hotel, Anglesea Street, Temple Bar,D2 ☎01 6715622 N
Blooms Hotel, Fleet Street, D2 ☎01 6708122***
Burlington Hotel, Upper Leeson Street, Ballsbridge, D4 ☎01 6605222****

Buswells Hotel, Molesworth Street, D2 ☎01 6146500 N
Central Hotel, Exchequer Street, D2 ☎01 6797302 ***
Clarence Hotel, Wellington Quay, D2 ☎01 6709000 U
Conrad Hotel, Earlsfort Terrace, D2 ☎01 6765555 *****
Davenport Hotel, Merrion Square, D2 ☎01 7073500 U
Earl of Kildare Hotel, Kildare Street, D2 ☎01 6794388 *
Georgian House Hotel, Lower Baggot Street, D2 ☎01 6618832 ***

Grafton Plaza, Johnston's Place, D2 ☎01 4750888 ***
Harding Hotel, Copper Alley, Christchurch, D2 ☎01 6796500 **
Hibernian Hotel, Eastmoreland Place, Ballsbridge, D4 ☎01 6687666 U
Jurys Hotel and Towers, Pembroke Road, Ballsbridge, D4 ☎01 6605000 *****
Jurys Christchurch Inn, Christchurch Place, D8 ☎01 4540000 ***
Kelly's Hotel, 32 South Great George's Street, D2 ☎01 6779277 *

Lansdowne Hotel, 27/29
Pembroke Road, D4
☎01 6682522 * *
Leeson Court,
Lower Leeson Street, D2
☎01 6763380 * *
Longfield's Hotel,
Fitzwilliam Street, D2
☎01 6761367 * * *
Mespil Hotel,
Mespil Road, D2
☎01 6671222 * * *
Mont Clare Hotel,
Merrion Square, D2
☎01 6073800 * * *
Russell Court Hotel,
Harcourt Street, D2
☎01 4784066 * * *
Sachs Hotel,
Morehampton Road,
Donnybrook, D4
☎01 6680995 * * *
Shelbourne Hotel,
St Stephen's Green, D2
☎01 6766471 * * * * *
Stephen's Hall Hotel,
Lower Leeson Street, D2
☎01 6610585 * * *
Temple Bar Hotel,
Fleet Street, D2
☎01 6773333 * * *
The Aston Hotel,
Aston Quay, D2
☎01 6779300 N
Wellington Hotel, 21-22
Wellington Quay, D2
☎01 6779315 R
Westbury Hotel,
off Grafton Street, D2
☎01 6791122 * * * *

North City Hotels (within 3 km of O'Connell Street)

Ashling Hotel,
Parkgate Street, D8
☎01 6772324 * * *
Barry's Hotel,
Great Denmark Street, D1
☎01 8746943 * *
Cassidy's,
7-8 Cavendish Row, D1
☎01 8780555 * * *
Clifton Court Hotel,
O'Connell Bridge, D1
☎01 8743535 * *
Dergvale Hotel,
4 Gardiner Place, D1
☎01 8744753 * *
Gresham Hotel,
O'Connell Street, D1
☎01 8746881 * * * *
Jury's Custom House Inn,
Custom House Quay, D1
☎01 6075000 *
Maple Hotel, 75 Lower
Gardiner Street, D1
☎01 8740225 * *

North Star Hotel,
Amiens Street, D 1
☎01 8363136 * *
Royal Dublin Hotel,
O'Connell Street, D1
☎01 8733666 * * *
Wynns Hotel,
Lower Abbey Street, D1
☎01 8745131 R

South Dublin Hotels (seaside and suburbs)

Court Hotel,
Killiney, Co. Dublin
☎01 2851622 * * *
Fitzpatrick Castle Hotel,
Killiney, Co. Dublin
☎01 2840700 * * * * *
Hotel Pierre,
3 Victoria Terrace,
Dun Laoghaire
☎01 2800291 * *
Doyle Montrose Hotel,
Stillorgan Road, Co. Dublin
☎01 2693311 * * *
**Kilternan Golf & Country
Club Hotel,**
Kilternan, Co. Dublin
☎01 2955559 U
Kingston Hotel,
Adelaide Street,
Dun Laoghaire
☎01 2801810 * *
Orwell Lodge Hotel, 77
Orwell Road, Rathgar, D6
☎01 4977258
Rathmines Plaza Hotel,
Lr Rathmines Road, D6
☎01 4966966 * * *
Royal Marine Hotel,
Marine Road, Dun
Laoghaire
☎01 2801911 * * *
Stillorgan Park Hotel,
Stillorgan, Co. Dublin
☎01 2881621 * * *
Doyle Tara Hotel,
Merrion Road, Co. Dublin
☎01 2694666 * * *
Rochestown Lodge Hotel,
Rochestown Avenue,
Dun Laoghaire
☎01 2853555 * * *

North Dublin Hotels (seaside and suburbs)

Deer Park Hotel,
Howth, Co. Dublin
☎01 8322624 * * *
Doyle Skylon Hotel,
Upper Drumcondra Road,
D9 ☎01 8379121 * * *
Forte Posthouse Dublin,
Dublin Airport
☎01 8080500 * * * *

Forte Travelodge,
Pinnock Hill, Swords
Roundabout, Belfast Road,
Co. Dublin
☎01 8409233 U
Grand Hotel,
Malahide, Co. Dublin
☎01 8450000 * * * *
Grove Hotel, Grove Road,
Malahide, Co. Dublin
☎01 8452208 *
Hollybrook Hotel,
Hollybrook Park,
Clontarf, D3
☎01 8336623 * *
Howth Lodge Hotel,
Howth, Co. Dublin
☎01 8321010 * * *
Marine Hotel,
Sutton, D13
☎01 8390000 * * *
Park Lodge Hotel,
7 North Circular Road, D7
☎01 8386428 *
Pier House Hotel,
The Harbour, Skerries,
Co. Dublin
☎01 8491708 *
**Portmarnock Hotel & Golf
Links,** Strand Road,
Portmarnock, Co. Dublin
☎01 8460611 * * * *
Regency Hotel,
Swords Road,
Whitehall, D9
☎01 8373544 * * *
Saint Lawrence Hotel,
Harbour Road, Howth,
Co. Dublin
☎01 8322643 * *
Sands Hotel,
Coast Road, Portmarnock,
Co. Dublin
☎01 8460003 * *
Stuart Hotel,
Coast Road, Malahide,
Co. Dublin
☎01 8450099 * *
Sutton Castle Hotel,
Red Rock, Sutton,
Co. Dublin
☎01 8322688 * * *

West Dublin Hotels

Doyle Green Isle Hotel,
Naas Road, Dublin 22
☎01 4593406 * * *
**Finnstown Country House
& Golf Course,**
Lucan, Co. Dublin
☎01 6280644 * * *
Spa Hotel,
Lucan, Co. Dublin
☎01 6280494 * *
West County Hotel,
Chapelizod, Co. Dublin
☎01 6264647 * *

Southside Guesthouses/B&Bs

Aberdeen Lodge,
53 Park Avenue, Ailesbury
Road, Ballsbridge, D4
☎01 2838155
Anglesea Town House,
63 Anglesea Road,
Ballsbridge, D4
☎01 6683877
Ariel House,
52 Lansdowne Road, D4
☎01 6685512
Beddington,
181 Rathgar Road, D6
☎01 4978047
Belgrave Guesthouse,
8-10 Belgrave Square, D6
☎01 4962549
Carrick Hall,
69 Orwell Road, Rathgar, D6
☎01 4922444
Cedar Lodge,
98 Merrion Road, D4
☎01 6684410
Clara House,
23 Leinster Road,
Rathmines, D6
☎01 4975904
Eglington Manor,
83 Eglington Road,
Donnybrook, D4
☎01 2693273
Fitzwilliam,
41 Fitzwilliam Street
Upper, D2
☎01 6600448
Glenogra House,
64 Merrion Road,
Ballsbridge, D4
☎01 6683661
Glenveagh Townhouse,
31 Northumberland Road,
Ballsbridge, D4
☎01 6684612
Grafton House,
26 South Great George's
Street, D2
☎01 6792041
**Grey Door
Residence/Restaurant,**
22 Upper Pembroke St,
D2
☎01 6763286
Kilronan House,
70 Adelaide Road, D2
☎01 4755266
Lansdowne Lodge,
6 Lansdowne Terrace,
Shelbourne Road, D4
☎01 6605755
Lansdowne Manor,
46-48 Lansdowne Road,
D4
☎01 6603533
**Mount Herbert
Guesthouse,**
7 Mount Herbert Road,
Ballsbridge, D4
☎01 6684321

Merrion Hall,
54 Merrion Road,
Ballsbridge, D4
☎01 6681426
Number Eighty-Eight,
88 Pembroke Road, D4
☎01 6600277
Raglan Lodge,
10 Raglan Road,
Ballsbridge, D4
☎01 6606697
Sandycove Guesthouse,
Sandycove Seafront,
Co. Dublin
☎01 2841600
Staunton's on the Green,
83 St Stephen's Green, D2
☎01 4782300
St Aidan's Guesthouse,
32 Brighton Road,
Rathgar, D6
☎01 4902011

Northside Guesthouses/B&Bs

Anchor Guesthouse,
49 Lower Gardiner Street,
D1
☎01 8786913
Carmel House,
16 Upper Gardiner Street,
D1
☎01 8741639
Charleville Lodge,
268-272 North Circular
Road, D7
☎01 8386633
Clifden House,
32 Gardiner Place, D1
☎01 8746364
Dorchester House,
69 North Circular Road,
D7
☎01 8385204
Egan's,
7 Iona Park, Glasnevin, D9
☎01 8303611
Harvey's Guesthouse,
11 Upper Gardiner Street,
D1
☎01 8748384
Iona House,
5 Iona Park, Glasnevin, D9
☎01 8306217
Marian Guesthouse,
21 Upper Gardiner Street,
D1
☎01 8744129
Othello House,
74 Lower Gardiner Street,
D1
☎01 8555442
Phoenix Park House,
38 Parkgate Street, D8
☎01 6772870
St Andrew's Guesthouse,
1 Lambay Road,
Drumcondra, D9
☎01 8374684

Talbot Guesthouse,
95-98 Talbot Street, D1
☎01 8749202

West Dublin Guesthouses

**Kingswood Country
House & Restaurant,**
Naas Road,
Clondalkin, D22
☎01 4592428
Westlink Lodge,
Palmerstown Village, D22
☎01 6235494

Northside Hostels

Abbey Hostel,
29 Bachelor's Walk, D1
☎01 8780700
Abraham's House,
82-83 Gardiner Street, D1
☎01 8550600
Charles Stewart,
5-6 Parnell Sq. East, D1
☎01 8780350
**Globetrotters Tourist
Hostel,**
46 Lower
Gardiner Street, D1
☎01 8735893
Isaac's,
Frenchman's Lane, near
Busarus
☎01 8556215
Join My Way,
15 Talbot Street, D1
☎01 8788484
Marlborough Hostel,
81-82 Marlborough
Street, D1
☎01 8747629

Southside Hostels

Ashfield House,
19/20 D'Olier Street, D2
☎01 6797734
Avalon House,
55 Aungier Street, D2
☎01 4750001
Brewery Hostel,
22 Thomas Street, D8
☎01 4538600
Kinlay House,
Lord Edward Street, D2
☎01 6796644
Morehampton House,
78 Morehampton
Road, D4
☎01 6688866
**Oliver St John Gogarty
Temple Bar Hostel,**
19-21 Anglesea Street, D2
☎01 6711822

DIRECTORY

Places To Eat In Dublin

Dublin has come on in leaps and bounds in terms of both the number and the quality of mid-priced and top-of-the-range restaurants. Reflecting the city's coming of age and its re-emergence as an important European capital, restaurateurs representing a wealth of cultures and traditions in the preparation of food have opened restaurants where before there was a shoeshop or a newsagents or any number of failed retail enterprises on poorly trading streets. Some of these streets have received an injection of life on account of this phenomenon, Dame Street and South Great George's Street being examples. These two streets, which join each other a few hundred metres west of Trinity College on Dame Street, play host to a variety of European, Eastern and Far Eastern eating establishments, and attract diners from all over Dublin. But they are also a magnet for many visitors to the city who now find they have a very wide choice available to them, and at a quality that often surprises them. Of course, let us not forget the many restaurants which offer a more traditional Irish fare. These too have increased in number and quality and have enhanced Dublin's reputation as a place in which you can eat extremely well. The vegetarian traveller will not be disappointed - at lunchtime in particular you can eat very well and inexpensively in a number of vegetarian restaurants and cafés around the city. In the evening, in response to the growing demand for a healthier diet, some restaurants will offer at least one vegetarian starter and main course on their 'a la carte' menu.

Apart from the Dame Street/George's Street axis, there are other districts in the city in which there is a growing number of restaurants within a stone's throw of each other. Temple Bar, for example, has over 40 restaurants in its narrow confines; the area around Grafton Street will not let you down in terms of choice and quality, especially if Italian or Indian cooking is to your liking. Don't be surprised to discover, though, that the city and suburbs are home to literally hundreds of restaurants and that, unlike the congregation of cooks in Dame Street and South Great George's Street, some of the unmissable restaurants in Dublin have to be sought out among the back streets and in the suburbs.

To summarise, if you want to eat superb food in exquisite surroundings, Dublin can provide, and handsomely. If you want to eat well but not spend more than £15, again Dublin will not let you down. If vegetarian fare is what you want, you will be rewarded with a surprisingly good choice (considering you are in a strong meat-eating culture). And if you want to grab an internationally recognised burger or chicken and chips, you will not have far to look. Finally, if you want to savour a pint or a glass of Guinness or any of the excellent Irish-brewed beers with your meal, an increasing number of pubs in Dublin are providing excellent fare at lunchtime, and some of them into the early evening.

Below is a list of some of the places we feel deserve recommendation, either because the food is superb, or the atmosphere is special, or it's a handy place to catch a quick bite. The list is selective and no doubt you will discover your own culinary gem. Eat well, and enjoy.

Places To Eat In Dublin City Centre

(All are open for lunch except where stated, and prices, where indicated, are approximate. For the purpose of this Eating Out Guide we have used the two canals as the natural boundary of the city centre.)

Ayumi-Ya Japanese Restaurant, 132 Lower Baggot Street, D2.
☎(01)6620233. Meat, fish and vegetarian food cooked in authentic Japanese style. Dinner £15+

Il Baccoro, Meeting House Square, Temple Bar, D2.
☎ (01)6714597. Dublin's first osteria, oozing with Italian atmosphere. Good house wine.

The Bistro, Castle Market, D2.
☎(01)6715430. Friendly, popular, reasonably priced – and good food. Lunch £5+ Dinner £12+

Blazing Salads, Powerscourt Townhouse, D2.
☎(01)6719552. Excellent vegetarian restaurant catering for (almost) all dietary requirements. Open Mon-Sat.

Not open in the evening. Lunch £4+

Botticelli, 3 Temple Bar, D2.
☎(01)6727289. Real Italian food in hugely popular restaurant. Lunch £8+ Dinner £15+

Bruno's, 30 East Essex Street, Temple Bar, D2.
☎ (01)6706767. Probably the classiest restaurant in Temple Bar. Lunch £12+ Dinner £25+

Cedar Tree Restaurant, 11A St Andrew Street, D2.
☎(01)6772121. A popular Lebanese restaurant with a

better than average selection of vegetarian dishes. Dinner £12+

Chameleon, 1 Lower Fownes Street, Temple Bar, D2. ☎(01)6710362. Well regarded and intimate, specialising in Indonesian cuisine. Dinner £15+

Chez Jules, D'Olier Street, D2. ☎(01) 6770499. Atmospheric French bistro in city centre and reasonably priced. Lunch £6+ Dinner £10+

Cooke's Restaurant, Castle Market, Opposite Powerscourt Townhouse, D2. ☎(01)6790536. One of the city's trendiest restaurant in attractive corner location. Lunch £15+ Dinner £25+

Commons Restaurant, 86 St Stephen's Green, D2. ☎(01)4752597. Upmarket restaurant in lavish Georgian townhouse basement. Lunch £20+ Dinner £35+

Cornucopia, 19 Wicklow Street, D2. ☎(01)6777583. Wholefood vegetarian restaurant open for breakfast, lunch and early dinner. Lunch £5+ Dinner £10+

Davy Byrne's Pub, 21 Duke Street, D2. ☎(01)6775217. Famous pub with James Joyce associations, specialises in seafood preparations. Lunch £8+ Dinner £12+

Dish, 2 Crow Street, Temple Bar, D2. ☎(01)6711248. Interesting and creative food in trendy establishment. Lunch £10+ Dinner £15+

Dobbin's, 15 Stephen's Lane, Mount Street, D2. ☎(01)6764679. Famous old Dublin bistro. Lunch £15+ Dinner £20+

Eastern Tandoori, 34/35 South William Street, D2. ☎(01)6710506. Always reliable ethnic restaurant off Grafton Street. Lunch £12+ Dinner £20+

Eden, Meeting House Square, Temple Bar, D2. ☎(01)6705372. One of the

few genuinely classy restaurants in Temple Bar, in attractive location. Lunch £12+ Dinner £20+

Fitzers, National Gallery, Merrion Square, D2. ☎(01)6614496. Popular lunchtime self-service restaurant serving a variety of interesting dishes. Lunch only and get there before 12.30. Lunch £8+. Fitzers also have restaurants on Dawson Street (6771155) and in the RDS in Ballsbridge (6671301). These are more upmarket and are open for evening meals.

Les Freres Jacques, 74 Dame Street, D2. ☎(01)6794555. French cuisine with accent on fresh fish and seasonal specialities. Lunch £15+ Dinner £25+

Govinda's Vegetarian Restaurant, 4 Aungier Street, D2. ☎(01)4750309. Standard vegetarian fare in very clean restaurant at a reasonable price. Lunch £4+ Dinner £6+

The Grey Door Restaurant, 22/23 Upper Pembroke Street, D2. ☎(01)6763286. Long-established restaurant specialising in Russian/Scandinavian dishes situated metres from Fitzwilliam Square. Lunch £10+ Dinner £20+

Juice, South Great George's Street, D2. ☎(01)4757856. Superb vegetarian cuisine in stylish environment. Mostly organic, including the wines. Great coffee and juices. Lunch £7+ Dinner £10+

Kilkenny Kitchen, Nassau Street, D2. ☎(01)6777066. Self-service restaurant overlooking the grounds of Trinity College with an excellent choice of salads, hot dishes and desserts. Lunch £5+ Not open in the evening

Mao, Chatham Row, D2. ☎(01)6704899. Asian cuisine at its most modern and most western in stylish and busy restaurant off Grafton Street. Lunch £7+ Dinner £10+

La Mère Zou, 22 St Stephen's Green, D2. ☎(01)6616669. Basement 'Brasserie Française' in Georgian house. Good food at a reasonable price. Lunch £10+ Dinner £15+

Mermaid Café, 69/70 Dame Street, D2. ☎(01)6708236. One of the city's best mid-priced restaurants. Interesting food, decent vegetarian choice. Lunch £6+ Dinner £12+

Little Caesar's Italian Restaurant, 5 Balfe Street, D2. ☎(01)6718714. Popular Italian restaurant off Grafton Street. Warm and friendly atmosphere. Lunch £7+ Dinner £12+

The Lord Edward, 23 Christchurch Place, D8. ☎(01)4542420. Dublin's oldest seafood restaurant, overlooking Christ Church Cathedral. Lunch £12+ Dinner £20+

Milano's, 38 Dawson Street & Temple Bar, D2. ☎(01)6707744. Bright, modern, busy and informal restaurant chain serving reliable but not exciting Italian fare. Lunch £7+ Dinner £10+

Mitchells Cellars, 21 Kildare Street, D2. ☎(01)6624724. A long-established, traditional, lunchtime-only restaurant in original wine cellars, situated a stone's throw from Dáil Éireann (Parliament) Lunch £10+

Monty's of Kathmandu, 28 Eustace Street, Temple Bar, D2. ☎(01)6704911. Nepalese cuisine is central to this Indian restaurant, one of the best places to eat in Temple Bar. Lunch £8+ Dinner £12+

Odessa, 13/14 Dame Court, D2. ☎(01)6707634. Young, trendy clientele in chic surroundings. Reasonable food at a reasonable price. Lunch £8+ Dinner £12+

101 Talbot, 101/102 Talbot Street, D1. ☎(01)8745011. Superb food at a reasonable price, combining creativity with reliability. Vegetarian and vegan dishes always available. Full bar. Lunch £6+ Dinner £10+

Pasta Fresca, 2-4 Chatham Street, D2. ☎(01)6792402. Fine Italian food in attractive surroundings beside Grafton Street. Lunch £7+ Dinner £12+

Peacock Alley, 109 St Stephen's Green, D2. ☎(01)6770708. Food is never dull in this popular and highly regarded restaurant. Lunch £10+ Dinner £20+

QV2 Restaurant, 14/15 St Andrew Street, D2. ☎(01)6773363. Stylish and popular restaurant a stone's throw from the main tourist office. Lunch £8+ Dinner £15+

Rajdoot Tandoori, 26-28 Clarendon Street, D2. ☎(01)6794274. Established Indian restaurant behind the Westbury Hotel. Lunch £10+ Dinner £20+

Restaurant Patrick Guilbaud, 21 Upper Merrion Street, D2. ☎(01)6764192. The French restaurant in Dublin. If stylish French cuisine is your thing, look no further. Lunch £20+ Dinner £25+

Shalimar, 17 South Great George's Street, D2. ☎(01)6710738. Indian restaurant specialising in Tandoori and Balti. Informal atmosphere. Lunch £8+ Dinner £12+

The Tea Room, Clarence Hotel, Temple Bar, D2. ☎(01)6707766. Stylish food in stylish surroundings. One of the city's trendiest restaurants housed in the most chic hotel of them all. Lunch £15+ Dinner £25+

Tosca, 20 Suffolk Street, D2. ☎(01)6796744. South European cuisine in city centre. Imaginative food served in a pleasant ambience. Lunch £7+ Dinner £12+

Trastevere, Temple Bar Square, D2. ☎(01)6708343. You can eat well and at a reasonabe price in this bright and airy restaurant looking onto Temple Bar Square. Lunch £7+ Dinner £12+

Trocadero Restaurant, 3 St Andrew Street, D2. ☎(01)6775545. An unassuming restaurant with a very loyal clientele. Famous for its late-night revellers. Dinner £20+

The Winding Stair, 40 Ormond Quay, D1. ☎(01)8733292. Soups and sandwiches and good coffee in rambling old secondhand bookshop. Views across the river. Closed at night-time.

Yamamori, South Great George's Street, D2. ☎(01)4755001. Japanese noodles served in lively restaurant frequented by young trendies. Go for the atmosphere, the food is secondary. Lunch £6+ Dinner £8+

Restaurants Outside The City Centre

North

Abbey Tavern, Abbey Street, Howth, Co. Dublin. ☎(01)8390307. Seafood a speciality in this 16th-century-style tavern and restaurant. Traditional music is a feature here. Dinner £20+

The King Sitric , East Pier, Howth, Co. Dublin. ☎(01)8325235. Famous for its seafood, landed daily on Howth Pier. Long-established and very popular. Dinner £28+

Old Schoolhouse Restaurant, Swords, Co. Dublin. ☎(01)8402846. Established restaurant in a converted schoolhouse. Lunch £15+ Dinner £25+

South

Ayumi-Ya Japanese Restaurant, Newtownpark Avenue, Blackrock, Co. Dublin. ☎(01)2831767. Traditional Japanese cuisine with fish and meat dishes and a wide vegetarian choice. Dinner £20+

Beaufield Mews, Woodlands Avenue, Stillorgan, Co. Dublin. ☎(01)2880375. Stables, coach house and hay loft neatly converted into restaurants and lounges. A bit off the beaten track, but worth the trip. Dinner £15+

Brasserie Na Mara, 1 Harbour Road, Dun Laoghaire, Co. Dublin. ☎(01)2806767. Seafood a speciality in this attractive restaurant overlooking Dun Laoghaire harbour. Lunch £12+ Dinner £20+

Ernie's Restaurant, Mulberry Gardens, Donnybrook, D4. ☎(01)2693300. Tasteful surroundings enhance the fine cuisine in an out of the way restaurant with plenty of character. Lunch £12+ Dinner £20+

Escape, 1 Albert Avenue, Bray, Co. Wicklow. ☎(01)2866755. Established vegetarian restaurant just off Victorian seafront and 5 minutes' walk from DART. Lunch £6+ Dinner £10+

Kites Chinese Restaurant, 15/17 Ballsbridge Terrace, D4. ☎(01)6607415. Authentic Chinese restaurant. Lunch £12+ Dinner £22+

Langkawi, 46 Upper Baggot Street, D2. ☎(01)6682760. Deservedly popular Malaysian restaurant. Lunch £10+ Dinner £20

The Lobster Pot , 9 Ballsbridge Terrace, D4. ☎(01)6680025. Established seafood restaurant, close to many hotels and guesthouses in fashionable Ballsbridge district. Lunch £20+ Dinner £25+

Roly's Bistro, 7 Ballsbridge Terrace, D4. ☎(01)6682611. Highly popular restaurant in fashionable Ballsbridge district. Reservation essential for lunch and dinner. Lunch £12+ Dinner £25+

Señor Sassi's, 146 Upper Leeson Street, D4. ☎(01)6684544. Mediterranean cuisine at a reasonable price in popular restaurant. Lunch £8+ Dinner £15+

Thai House, Dalkey, Co. Dublin. ☎ (01)2847304. Regarded by many as the best Thai restaurant in Dublin. Take a trip on the DART and see for yourself. Dinner only £12+

DIRECTORY
Shopping In Dublin

Since the creation of pedestrian zones in two distinct areas of the city, shopping has become a much more pleasurable experience. The two main shopping streets, **Grafton Street** on the south side and **Henry Street** on the north side, are both pedestrian streets and thriving as a result. On Grafton Street you will find the upmarket **Brown Thomas** and the newly-opened **Marks and Spencer**. Not to be outdone, Henry Street is home to **Arnotts** and **Roches Stores**, two large stores in which you will be able to choose from a wide range of goods. On **O'Connell Street**, there is the imposing **Clery's** department store, a traditional establishment which has traded from this historic building since 1883. Other large stores are **Penneys** on Henry Street and O'Connell Street, **Marks and Spencer** on Henry Street and Grafton Street, and the various department stores in the largest of the shopping centres.

Shopping centres are numerous throughout the city. Tucked away behind Grafton Street is one of the smallest and most interesting of these. The **Powerscourt Townhouse Centre**, converted from a stately Georgian mansion into an airy space bathed in natural light which filters through the glass roof, is full of small boutiques and craft shops, cafés, restaurants and art and craft galleries. Elsewhere, the **Stephen's Green Shopping Centre** is popular and has its own department store, and to the immediate east of Grafton Street is the upmarket shopping mall, the **Royal Hibernian Way**. On the north side of the city the busy **ILAC Centre** is host to a large number of shops and a department store, while the newly-opened **Jervis Street Shopping Mall** (main entrance on Henry Street) is Dublin city's most modern - and biggest - shopping centre.

There are many large shops which specialise in Irish-made goods. Among the best of these are **The Kilkenny Shop**, **Blarney Woollen Mills** and **House of Ireland**, all on Nassau Street, and the **Dublin Woollen Mills** on Ormond Quay. Don't ignore the small shops hidden away on side streets, for it is in these shops that you can often find exactly what you are looking for and at a price which pleases. One very civilised aspect of shopping in Dublin is the lack of hard selling you are likely to encounter in all the shops and stores in which you browse. 'Can I help you?' is about the strongest phrase you will hear, unlike in some countries where the hard sell is commonplace. This sense of respect for your privacy and the unwillingness to enter your personal space in an intrusive manner is what makes shopping in Dublin so enjoyable.

Shopping hours in Dublin are, in general, between 09.00 and 17.30 or 18.00, Monday to Saturday. Many centre-city shops open till 20.00 on Thursdays. Below is a selective list of shops in which you may find yourself browsing during your stay.

Antiques
The antique quarter is in **Francis Street** in the Liberties, but you will also find many antique shops dotted around the city, especially along the **Liffey Quays** and on some of the streets **near Grafton Street**.

Art
There is a large number of commercial art galleries around the city where you can view the work of Irish and international artists. You can find a comprehensive list of the city's galleries and the painters on show in the free Dublin Event Guide or the fortnightly In Dublin magazine. Bord Fáilte Information Sheet No. 37 also lists the commercial galleries.

Bookshops
Not surprisingly, in a city of writers, the reader is spoilt for choice when it comes to bookshops. Recommended ones are **Books Upstairs** on College Green, **Dublin Bookshop** on Grafton Street, **Eason's** on O'Connell Street, **Greene's** on Clare Street, **Fred Hanna** on Nassau Street, **Hodges Figgis** on Dawson Street, **Waterstone's** two branches in Dawson Street and the Jervis Centre, **Hughes & Hughes** in St Stephen's Green Centre and the **Library Shop** in Trinity College. Most suburban shopping centres also boast a good stockholding bookshop. Dozens of secondhand bookshops will be found all over the city.

Crafts
You can surround yourself with a huge range of crafts in some of the bigger shops, or you can quietly browse among the small shops and craft galleries. Tweeds, woollens, linen and lace, some of it made into stunning patterns and elegant shapes to wear, Aran sweaters, delicate, handcut jewellery, functional and artwork pottery, a unique range of Irish crystal - all can be found throughout the city. Well established and popular shops are **The Kilkenny Shop**, **Blarney Woollen Mills** and **House of Ireland**, all on Nassau Street, **The Craft Gallery** in the Powerscourt Townhouse Centre, **Tower Design Craft Centre** on Pearse Street, **Designyard** in Temple Bar, **Whichcraft** on Lord Edward Street, **Louis Mulcahy Pottery** on Dawson Street and the **Dublin Woollen Company** on Ormond Quay.

Fashion for Men
Some very stylish fashion

boutiques carry on a tradition of beautifully cut Irish woollen and tweed coats, suits, jackets, casual trousers and all the accessories. Some recommended boutiques for the fashion conscious man are **Louis Copeland** on Pembroke Street and on Capel Street, **Alias Tom** on Duke Lane, **The Kilkenny Shop**, **Blarney Woollen Mills**, **Kennedy & McSharry** and **Kevin & Howlin** on Nassau Street, **FX Kelly**, **A Wear**, **Club Tricot** and **Brown Thomas** on Grafton Street, **Michael Barrie** on Duke Street, **John Taylor** on Kildare Street and **Dublin Woollen Mills** on Ormond Quay.

Fashion for Women
There are many superb Irish designers creating both adventurous and sophisticated garments for seasonal wear, for casual wear and, of course, for evening wear. All the exclusive boutiques will stock garments from foreign and Irish designers. Some shops you should look out for are **A Wear, Airwave, Brown Thomas, Pamela Scott, Pia Bang, Richard Alan** – all on Grafton Street, **Cleo** on Kildare Street, **Monica John** on South Anne Street, **Platform** on Duke Lane, **The Kilkenny Shop** and **Blarney Woollen Mills** on Nassau Street, **An Táin** in Temple Bar, **Dublin Woollen Mills** on Ormond Quay and the numerous boutiques in the **Powerscourt Townhouse Centre**, **Westbury Mall** and Royal **Hibernian Way**.

Jewellers
Many craft shops sell a wide range of Irish-made jewellery, however specific places to check out are: **Designyard** and **Equinox** in Temple Bar, **Weir & Sons** on Grafton Street, **Tower Design Centre** on Pearse Street, **Whichcraft** on Lord Edward Street and numerous small outlets in and around the **Powerscourt Townhouse Centre**.

Markets
The Stephen's Green Shopping Centre was in the 1970s the location of Dublin's famous Dandelion Market. Since its closure no other market has been able to capture its quaint and cosy atmosphere, but maybe that is simply rampant nostalgia. What markets do exist in Dublin are interesting and well worth visiting, especially **Christchurch Festival Market**, behind Mother Red Caps Tavern on Back Lane, opposite Christ Church Cathedral and open Fri-Sun; **Blackrock Market** in Blackrock, Co. Dublin, open at weekends; **Iveagh Market** which on Saturdays extends down Francis Street; **Liberty Market** on Meath Street; open-air market every Saturday in **Meeting House Square** in Temple Bar; Organic Food Market at **Dublin Food Co-op**, St Andrew's Centre, Pearse Street, every Saturday; **Dublin Corporation Market** (fruit, fish, vegetables, flowers) behind the Four Courts; the **Leinster Market** in George's Street Arcade Mon-Sat; and the most famous of all, the fruit and vegetable traders on **Moore Street**.

Miscellaneous Shops
Of course, not fitting in to any of the standard categories of tourist-related shops are many shops which combine to make a shopping expedition a bit of an adventure. There are joke shops, £1 shops where every single item costs £1 or less, bargain-book shops, secondhand clothes shops, genealogy shops, and specialist shops for the connoisseur. Elsewhere, if it's an international adaptor you want, or an umbrella to replace the one you left in - was it Trinity College or St Patrick's Cathedral? - or a pair of sunglasses because you didn't think the sun shone in Ireland, Dublin shops will be able to provide.

Records and Musical Instruments
Dublin has an unusually large number of record shops for a city with a population of one million. The largest shops dealing in all musical tastes are **HMV** on Grafton Street and Henry Street, **Virgin Megastore** on Aston Quay, the **Golden Disc** shops on Grafton Street, North Earl Street, Liffey Street and the ILAC Centre, and **Tower Records** on Wicklow Street. **Claddagh Records** on Cecilia Street in the Temple Bar is a specialist traditional and folk music outlet.
If you are interested in buying a tin whistle, guitar, fiddle, accordion, flute, bodhran, or any of the other instruments which you might hear being played in the traditional music venues around town, there are a number of shops which will be able to help you out. Recommended shops for musical instruments are **Walton's Musical Galleries** on North Frederick Street, **Musicmaker** on Mary's Abbey, off Capel Street, **Musicmaker** on Exchequer Street, **McNeill's** on Capel Street and **Rock Steady Music** on Chatham Place.

Woollens
The large shops which specialise in Irish-made woollen goods have been mentioned above. Smaller shops worth visiting are **The Sweater Shop** on Wicklow Street, **Monaghan's** in the Grafton Street Arcade, **Cleo** on Kildare Street, **Inish** on Lord Edward Street, and the numerous small shops hidden away off Grafton Street.

Drinks
If you have any money left after the extravagance of the above, perhaps treat yourself or someone back home to a bottle of a famous Irish drink. Suggestions for gifts to bring home are the numerous Irish whiskeys (Jamesons, Paddy, John Power, Old Bushmills, Black Bush, Tullamore Dew, Crested Ten), Baileys Irish Cream Liqueur, Irish Mist, a bottle of porter (Guinness, Darcy's or Porter House), Carolans Irish Cream Liqueur. Savour them in your own time in a Dublin pub before deciding on the one to suit your palate.

DIRECTORY
Entertainment In Dublin

From suave cabarets with a distinctly Irish flavour in comfortable banqueting halls which seat several hundred people, to small pubs in the city centre where a fiddler and a flautist play almost unnoticed in the corner, the choices of being entertained in Dublin are many and wide.

Traditional Music

We start with music, and because traditional music is so deeply engrained in Irish culture, it is here we begin our entertainment guide. The most common place to hear live traditional music (trad) is in a pub, but you should also check any of the regular 'listings' in the evening newspapers or the 'event guides' (see *Essential Visitor Information* - newspapers section). Below is a list of the pubs in which traditional musicians regularly perform. Some pubs arrange for the musicians to play, others simply keep some seats in the pub free and if the musicians come there will be music and if they don't, well they are probably playing somewhere else or simply taking a night off. Read *A Tour of Dublin Pubs* on pages 79-84 for more information on the pubs mentioned below. With regard to etiquette in pubs where there are musicians playing for free, no publican will appreciate the music enthusiast who comes to listen to the music but who does not buy a drink. So, to avoid bad feeling, get a drink early on and enjoy the music.

The Barnowl, James's Street, D8. Informal sessions. No cover charge.
The Brazen Head, Bridge Street, D8.
☎ (01)6779549. Regular music, no charge.
The Cobblestone, Smithfield, D7. Regular gigs, occasional cover charge.

Eamonn Dorans, Crown Alley, Temple Bar, D2.
☎ (01)6799114. Music most evenings.
The Ferryman, 35 Sir John Rogerson's Quay, D2. ☎ (01)6717053. Music most nights of the week. No charge.
Fitzsimons, Essex Street, Temple Bar, D2.
☎ (01)6779315. Regular music and set dancing.
Harcourt Hotel, 60 Harcourt Street, D2.
☎ (01)4783677. Regular sessions (no charge) and concerts with entrance charge.
Hughes, 19 Chancery Street, D7.
☎ (01)8726540. Music and set dancing. No charge.
Keating's, corner of Abbey Street and Jervis Street, D1.
☎ (01)8731567. Regular music. No charge.
Mother Red Caps Tavern, Back Lane, D8.
☎ (01)4538306. Regular concerts with entrance charge.
O'Donoghue's, 15 Merrion Row, D2.
☎ (01)6607194. Regular music. No charge.
Oliver St John Gogarty's, Temple Bar, D2.
☎ (01)6711822
O'Shea's Merchant, 12 Lower Bridge Street, D8.
☎ (01)6793797. Regular music and set dancing. No charge.
Searson's, 42 Upper Baggot Street, D4.
☎ (01)6600330. Phone for details.
Slattery's, 129 Capel Street, D1.
☎ (01)8727971. Regular music and occasionally set dancing. No charge. Regular concerts upstairs with entrance charge.

Trinity Inn, 37b Pearse Street, D2.
☎ (01)6792860. Serious traditional singing club every Friday night. Strictly no talking during the songs. No charge.
Whelan's, 16 Wexford Street, D2.
☎ (01)4780766. Regular concerts with entrance charge.

Classical

The **National Concert Hall** has a complete programme of mainly classical performances throughout the year. It also puts on regular lunchtime recitals which cost around £5. Other regular classical venues are listed below.

National Concert Hall, Earlsfort Terrace, south of St Stephen's Green.
☎ (01)4751572
Bank of Ireland Arts Centre on Foster Place (beside College Green).
☎ (01)6711488. Lunchtime recitals.
Hugh Lane Municipal Gallery of Modern Art on Parnell Square.
☎(01)8741903. Sunday concerts.
Royal Hospital Kilmainham.
☎ (01)6718666. Occasional concerts.

Rock and Country Music

Apart from the major rock and country concerts which take place in the RDS, Point Depot and the National Stadium and for which you may need to buy a ticket many weeks, if not months, in advance, there are many smaller venues around the city and in the suburbs where you can catch rock and country musicians and bands playing to a live audience. Check the evening newspapers and the event guides. The major record stores act as agents for most of the big concerts. The venues listed below are among the most popular in the city at time of writing.

Bad Bob's Backstage Bar, East Essex Street, D2. ☎ (01)6775482. Popular venue for country and rock bands. Late opening with bar. Entrance charge.
Barry's Hotel, Great Denmark Street, D1. ☎ (01)8746943. Regular country music venue off Parnell Square. Entrance charge.
Break for the Border, Stephen Street Lower, D2. ☎ (01)4780300. Popular late-night venue for live bands. Entrance charge.
Bruxelles, 7 Harry Street (off Grafton Street), D2. ☎ (01)6799636. Regular live acts.
DA Club, Clarendon Market, D2. ☎ (01)6711130. Regular gigs. Entrance charge.
Eamonn Dorans, Crown Alley, D2. ☎ (01)6799114. Live bands most nights in the heart of Temple Bar. Entrance charge.
Fitzsimons, Essex Street, Temple Bar, D2. ☎ (01)6779315. Regular live music. Cover charge.
International Bar, Wicklow Street, D2. ☎ (01)6779250. Small, atmospheric venue above famous pub. Entrance charge.
IFC, 6 Eustace Street, D2. ☎ (01)6793477. Late night gigs at the Irish Film Centre. Entrance charge.
Johnny Fox's, Glencullen, Co. Dublin. ☎ (01)2955647. Regular music in reputably Ireland's highest pub, up

in the Dublin mountains.
Mean Fiddler, Wexford Street, D2. ☎ (01)4758555. One of London's most successful live music venues is now in Dublin. Nightly concerts. Entrance charge.
Mother Red Caps Tavern, Back Lane, D8. ☎ (01)4538306. Rock and country concerts from time to time in lively and atmospheric venue. Entrance charge.
Olympia Theatre, Dame Street, D2. ☎ (01)6777744. Regular series of 'Midnight At The Olympia' live weekend concerts during the summer and intermittently during the winter. Also other regular concerts. Late bar. Entrance charge.
Red Box, 35 Harcourt Street, D2. ☎ (01)4780225. New venue already booking well-known bands. Entrance charge.
SFX, 28 Upper Sherrard Street, D1. ☎ (01)8745227. Long-established and popular venue for live bands. Entrance charge.
Slattery's, 129 Capel Street, D1. ☎(01)8727971. Mainly traditional but occasional rock and country. Entrance charge to concerts.
Temple Bar Music Centre, Curved Street, D2. ☎ (01)6790533. Popular live venue. Entrance charge.
Vicar Street, Thomas Street, D8. ☎ (01)6097788. New and popular live venue with busy calendar of gigs. Entrance charge.
Whelan's, 16 Wexford Street, D2. ☎ (01)4780766. Good venue for live acts, from trad to rock. Entrance charge.

Jazz and Blues

Several venues have carved out a name for themselves in either the live jazz or blues scene. Telephone to find out which are the jazz or blues nights.

Bruxelles, 7 Harry Street, (off Grafton Street) D2. ☎ (01)6799636.
Conrad Hotel, Earlsfort Terrace, D2. ☎ (01)6765555.
Harcourt Hotel, 60 Harcourt Street, D2. ☎ (01)4783677.
Hotel Pierre, Seafront, Dun Laoghaire. ☎ (01)2800291.
International Bar, Wicklow Street, D2. ☎ (01)6779250.
JJ Smyths, 12 Aungier Street, D2. ☎ (01)2472565.
Late at the Gaiety, South King Street, D2. ☎ (01)6773614.
McDaid's Pub, 3 Harry Street, D2. ☎ (01)6794395.
Reynard's, South Frederick Street, D2. ☎ (01)6775876.
Sach's Hotel, 19/29 Morehampton Road, Donnybrook, D4. ☎ (01)6680995.
Slattery's, 129 Capel Street, D1. ☎ (01)8727971.

Cabaret

An evening's entertainment at an Irish cabaret usually means a mixture of Irish song and dance and plenty of jokes. Some of the shows include dinner while some offer dinner as an option. A popular cabaret is Jury's Irish Cabaret, with 2$\frac{1}{2}$ hours of entertainment, 6 evenings a week from May to October. There have been Irish cabarets here for over 30 years.

Abbey Tavern, Howth, Co. Dublin. ☎ (01)8390307.
Clontarf Castle, Castle Avenue, Clontarf, D3. ☎ (01)8332321.
Doyle's Irish Cabaret, Burlington Hotel, Upper Leeson Street, D4. ☎ (01)6605222.
Jury's Irish Cabaret, Jury's Hotel, Ballsbridge, D4. ☎ (01)6605000.

Comedy

If you feel like a laugh, well Dublin wit is alive and well at several stand-up comedy venues. It may not be to your taste - that's a chance you take - but by and large you'll come away laughing. Telephone all venues to check what nights the comedy is on.

Halfpenny Bridge Inn, Temple Bar, D2. ☎ (01)6770616.
International Bar, Wicklow Street, D2. ☎ 6779250.
Irish Film Centre, 6 Eustace Street, Temple Bar, D2. ☎ (01)6795744.
Murphy's Laughter Lounge, Eden Quay, D1. ☎ 1800 266339 or 8744611.
The Norseman, Temple Bar, D2. ☎ (01)6715153.

Cinema

Ireland has the largest cinema-going audience in Europe in terms of its population. During the nineties, multi-plex cinemas have been opening all over Dublin, showing the leading films of the day. Unfortunately, there hasn't been a similar development in Arthouse Cinema, so the range of films on offer on any night of the week in the city centre is relatively narrow. The Irish Times is probably the best newspaper to get for cinema listings, but the

Evening Herald and the Dublin Event Guide also print cinema listings.

Centre City Cinemas

Ambassador, Parnell Square, D1. ☎ (01)8727000. 1 screen in converted theatre.
Savoy, O'Connell Street, D1. ☎ (01)8746000 for advance booking. 5 screens.
Screen, D'Olier Street, D2. ☎ (01)6714988. 3 screens.
Irish Film Centre (IFC), Eustace Street, D2. ☎ (01)6793477. 2 screens. Short-term membership available.
Virgin Cinemas, Parnell Street, D1. ☎ (01)8728400. 9 screen multiplex.

Suburban Cinemas

Bray Royal Cineplex. ☎ (01)2868686. Southside cinema, 18 km from Dublin.
Classic, Harolds Cross. ☎ (01)4923699. Southside cinema.
Forum Dun Laoghaire. ☎ (01)2300700. Southside cinema.
Ormonde Stillorgan. ☎ (01)2780000. Southside cinema.
Stella Rathmines. ☎ (01)4971281. Southside cinema.
Santry Omniplex. ☎ (01)8428844. Multi-screen cinema on northside.
UCI Blandchardstown. ☎1850 525354. Multi-screen cinema on westside.
UCI Coolock. ☎(01)8485122. Multi-screen cinema on northside.
UCI Tallaght. ☎ (01)4598400. Multi-screen cinema on southside.

Theatre

The Abbey Theatre is Ireland's National Theatre and there is always a strong presence of Irish plays in its annual season of drama. The Peacock Theatre, attached to the Abbey, devotes some of its season to new Irish playwrights. The Gate Theatre can always be relied upon to present powerful plays by both Irish and international playwrights. The Gaiety presents a more popular Irish drama, in the best sense of the term. It also hosts the Dublin Grand Opera season, the incredibly popular Christmas pantomimes and a variety of musical and theatrical entertainment. There are many other theatres, some of which present challenging drama to an interested theatre-going public and others whose programme is a more popular one. Whatever aspect of theatre you enjoy there will probably be something to interest you while you are in Dublin. For all up-to-date listings on what's on in the theatre world, consult the evening newspapers or any of the event guides.

Abbey Theatre, Abbey Street Lower, D1. ☎ (01)8787222.
Andrew's Lane Theatre, off Exchequer Street, D2. ☎ (01)6795720.
City Arts Centre, 23/25 Moss Street (opposite Custom House), D2. ☎ (01)6770643.
Focus Theatre, 6 Pembroke Place, D2. ☎ (01)6763071.
Gaiety Theatre, South King Street, D2. ☎ (01)6771717.
Gate Theatre, Parnell Square East, D1. ☎(01)8744045/8746042.

Olympia Theatre, Dame Street, D2.
☎ (01)6778962. (Ticket Office 6777744).
Peacock Theatre, address and phone number as Abbey Theatre.
Project Arts Centre, 39 Essex Street East, Temple Bar, D2. ☎ (01)6712321. (Under re-construction at time of writing)
Samuel Beckett Centre, Trinity College, D2.
☎ (01)6082461.
Tivoli Theatre, Francis Street, D8.
☎ (01)4544472/3.

A wide range of pubs and other, sometimes unusual, venues play host to many kinds of theatrical groups during the year. Among these venues are:
Bewley's Oriental Café, Grafton Street, D2.
☎ (01)6713387.
The Crypt Bar Centre, Dublin Castle, D2.
☎ (01)6713387.
International Bar, Wicklow Street, D2.
☎ (01)6779250.
Lambert Puppet Theatre, 5 Clifton Terrace, Monkstown, Co. Dublin.
☎ (01)2800974.
McDaid's Pub, off Grafton Street, D2.
☎ (01)6794395.

The Club Scene
The Georgian houses of Lower Leeson Street, busy office environments during the daytime, are transformed into Dublin's busiest nightclub scene by night. Elsewhere, around the Temple Bar district, clubs are springing up and the place is swinging with music from rock to ramba. Then there are the truly trendy clubs like the **POD, The Kitchen** and **Lillie's Bordello**, where music and film celebrities pop in and out, and the gear is decidedly flamboyant. The choice is yours. Check the

event guides for information on the clubs so you'll know what kind of dancing will be expected of you. Finally, have a good night out! Most of the late-night clubs on Leeson Street do not apply a cover charge but you are expected to buy a bottle of the over-priced and generally poor quality wine. Most clubs on Leeson Street serve meals. There are no live bands, most of the music is a disco sound and you probably won't get in if you're wearing denims. Some other clubs:
Annabels, Burlington Hotel, Upper Leeson Street, D4.
☎ (01)6605222.
Bad Bob's Backstage Bar, East Essex Street, Temple Bar, D2.
☎ (01)6792992. (under re-construction at time of writing)
Break for the Border, Stephen Street Lower, D2.
☎ (01)4780300. Live bands Wed-Sat with full bar till 02.00.
Club Paradiso, Irish Film Centre, Eustace Street, Temple Bar, D2.
☎ (01)6793477.
The Court, Harcourt Hotel, Harcourt Street, D2.
☎ (01)4783677.
DA Club, Clarendon Market, D2.
☎ (01)6711130.
Eamonn Dorans, Crown Alley, Temple Bar, D2.
☎ (01)6799114.
The Dungeon, Fitzpatrick's Castle Hotel, Killiney, Co. Dublin. ☎ (01)2840700.
Gigis, Russell Court Hotel, 21 Harcourt Street, D2.
☎(01)4784066.
The Kitchen, Clarence Hotel, 6-8 Wellington Quay or East Essex Street, Temple Bar, D2.
☎ (01)6776635.
Lillie's Bordello, Adam Court, Grafton Street, D2.
☎ (01)6799204.

The Loft, Purty Kitchen, Old Dun Laoghaire Road, Co. Dublin.
☎ (01)2843576.
Mean Fiddler, Wexford Street, D2.
☎ (01)4758555.
Howl at the Moon, Basement of O'Dwyer's Pub, 7 Lower Mount Street, D2.
☎ (01)6762887.
The Pier, Wellington Hotel, Temple Bar, D2.
☎ (01)6779315.
POD, Harcourt Street, D2.
☎ (01)4780166.
Raffles, Sachs Hotel, 19-29 Morehampton Road, Donnybrook, D4.
☎ (01)6680995.
Republica, Kildare Street, D2.
Reynards, South Frederick Street, D2.
☎(01)6775876.
Ri-Ra, Dame Court, D2.
☎(01)6774835.
The River Club, 48 Wellington Quay, D2.
☎ (01)6772382
Rumours, 19 O'Connell Street, D1.
☎ (01)8722850.
Velure, Gaiety Theatre, South King Street, D2.
☎ (01)6771717.

Miscellaneous
Cultúrlann na hÉireann, Belgrave Square, Monkstown, Co. Dublin. Céilí every Friday at 21.00 hours. ☎ (01)2800295.
Jameson Literary Pub Crawl - an evening of readings, song and performance around the literary pubs of Dublin. Nightly from The Duke Pub on Duke Street at 19.30. ☎ (01)4540228.
Irish Music Pub Crawl. ☎ (01)4780191. Starting from the Oliver St John Gogarty pub in Temple Bar and operating seven nights of the week between May and October.
Set Dancing at numerous locations throughout the city. Check the Dublin Event Guide for details.

105

DIRECTORY
Sporting Activities In Dublin

Dublin offers a wide variety of sporting activities throughout the year for both the spectator and the participant.

- as participant -

Golf

Golf is very popular in Ireland. There are superb courses all over the country and some of the most difficult and spectacular links courses in the world are to be found on Irish coasts. In Dublin, there are opportunities for the visitor to play on a number of 18-hole courses. Average green fees are in the region of £15 but can go as high as £50 for the top clubs. To play, most clubs simply require that you book in advance. *The Golfers' Guide to Ireland* can be purchased in most good bookshops and in any of the tourist offices. The Visitor Guide to Golfing in and around Dublin, published by Dublin Tourism, is available at all tourist offices for £1.50.

Tennis & Squash

Because of the inclement weather, the tennis season is relatively short. Despite this, there are dozens of private tennis clubs in Dublin and many of these are just a few kilometres from the city centre. You can play as a visitor in some of these clubs but most private clubs insist that visitors can only play if accompanied by a member. In contrast, the public tennis courts operate a first-come first-served (excuse the pun) basis. You can simply go along and pay for the number of hours you want to play. The playing surfaces are generally inferior to those of the private clubs but they are fine for the amateur player who doesn't mind the odd bad bounce. Some of the city's public parks have tennis courts, among them: Herbert Park in Ballsbridge; Bushy Park in Terenure; and St Anne's Park in Raheny. The only indoor courts in Dublin are those belonging to some

of the private clubs. Squash is a popular game in Dublin. All the clubs are private but you can phone **Squash Ireland** who have courts north and south of the Liffey:
Clontarf *(01-8331656)*; Dalkey *(01-2801515)*; Dartry *(01-4963910)* and Phoenix Park *(01-8385850)*. For information on badminton courts contact the Badminton Union of Ireland, Badminton Hall, Whitehall Road, Terenure, D12, Tel: *(01-4505966)* or *(01-4508101)*.

Swimming

Irish beaches, particularly those along the west coast, are clean by comparison to most European beaches. Even the beaches along Dublin Bay are relatively clean, considering the industrial and domestic activity along its shores. **Donabate** and **Portmarnock** on the north Dublin coastline are long, sandy beaches, as are **Booterstown** and **Blackrock** beaches on the south coastline. A popular bathing place during the summer months is off the pebbled **Killiney** beach, while beside the James Joyce Museum in **Sandycove** is Dublin's most famous bathing place, the formerly men-only and nudist **Forty-Foot**, although in recent years, due to pressure from women bathers, the men have backed off and now bathers of both gender can be seen diving in and out of the swell - with their togs on - except before 09.00 when nudist bathing is allowed. If the climate discourages you from donning your bathing suit and showing off your goosepimples - and let's face it, who could blame you - there are a number of public, indoor swimming pools around the city. Dublin could do with a few more, and of higher standard, but if you get the urge any one of the

pools below will allow you take the plunge. Telephone for swimming times.

Centre City Public Swimming Pools

Sean McDermott Street, D1. ☎(01)8720752
Marian Pool, beside Lansdowne Road Rugby Stadium, D4.
☎(01)6689539

Suburban Public Swimming Pools

Ballymun Shopping Centre, D11. ☎(01)8421368
Finglas, D11.
☎(01)8348005
Ballyfermot, D10.
☎(01)6266504
Northside Shopping Centre, Coolock, D5.
☎(01)8477743
Rathmines, D6.
☎(01)4961275
Willie Pearse Park, Crumlin, D12.
☎(01)4555792

Watersports
Sailing

You can go sailing from Dun Laoghaire Harbour on the south Dublin coast or from Howth Harbour on the north Dublin coast. There are yacht clubs in both of these sailing centres. You can also sail from Clontarf, Malahide, Rush and Skerries on the north side and other small coves along the coast. Contact the Irish Sailing Association, 3 Park Road, Dun Laoghaire, ☎*(01)2800239* for all the information you need. Bord Fáilte publishes a sailing information brochure as part of its *Only the Best* series, available at all tourist offices. Sailing courses are run regularly throughout the summer in a number of clubs. Try the Irish National Sailing School, 115 George's Street Lower, Dun Laoghaire, ☎*(01)2806654*, or the Fingal Sailing School, Upper Strand, Broadmeadow Estuary, Malahide, ☎*(01)8451979*.

Windsurfing

There is no shortage of wind to blow your sail in Ireland, and this sport would be much more popular were it not for the many cold and rainy days that put all but the keen enthusiast off braving the conditions. Down at the Grand Canal Dock in Ringsend you can windsurf from the **Surfdock Centre**, ☎*(01)6683945*. They run courses here, where the Grand Canal meets the Liffey. They have a fully stocked shop, with boards, wetsuits etc., and you can hire a board and sail by the hour.

Scuba Diving

If you are the underwater type you can be accommodated by **Oceantec**, 10/11 Marine Terrace, Dun Laoghaire, ☎*(01)2801083*, who hire out diving equipment for about £20 for a half-day. A local dive somewhere close to Dun Laoghaire costs £30. More information on scuba diving in Ireland can be obtained from the **Irish Underwater Council**, 78A Patrick Street, Dun Laoghaire, ☎*(01)2844607*.

Horse Riding

Ireland is famous for its horses and visitors come here each year to ride horses from the many equestrian and riding stables around the country. There are numerous horse-riding centres less than an hour's drive from Dublin. Bord Fáilte will provide you with a list of all the riding schools and stables in the country.

Cycling

The thundering rumble of the huge juggernauts as they trundle through the city can make for uncomfortable cycling. That said, there are thousands of regular cyclists in Dublin and, if you are fit and accustomed to cycling in traffic, there is no reason why you should

not hire a bicycle for a few days. On a bicycle you will be able to cover most of the city in a couple of days and you can also take a spin out along the coast or explore the Phoenix Park or either of the Dublin Canals. A word of caution: never leave your bike unlocked or with any kind of bag with belongings attached and unattended as there is a reasonable chance it will not be there when you get back. Consult the *Getting To And Around Dublin* section for information on bicycle hire.

Hill Walking

Apart from the city walks as described in this guide (see *Three Classic Walks*), there are lovely walks both north and south of the city. The most popular, and the one we would recommend, is **The Wicklow Way**. This runs south from Marley Park in the southern suburb of Rathfarnham, through the mountains of Wicklow to County Carlow - 132 km away. There are magnificent views along the Way, and if you have a few days to spend you could walk from Enniskerry to Glendalough, staying in the An Óige hostels en route:
Glencree (*01-2864037*); Knockree (*01-2864036*); Glenmalure (no phone) and Aughnavanagh (*0402-36366*). The path rises over 500 m for much of the route, so be prepared with warm and waterproof clothes, and do not travel alone as cloud and mist can descend rapidly. If you only have a day to spare you could take a Bus No. 44 from Hawkins Street (off Burgh Quay) to Enniskerry and walk to Powerscourt Waterfall. Another idea is to take the bus No. 44B from Hawkins Street to Glencullen. There are nice walks around this mountainous area and you can enjoy some liquid refreshment in Dublin's highest and very famous pub, Johnny Fox's.

- as spectator -

Gaelic Games

Gaelic Football and Hurling are two of the world's great field games. Hurling, in particular, is one of the fastest field games in the world. The **Gaelic Athletic Association (GAA)** presides over the sport in Ireland. Their headquarters are in Croke Park, Dublin 3, ☎*(01)8363222* and it is in this stadium every September that the two great Gaelic sporting events of the year take place, the Football and Hurling All-Ireland Finals. As a visitor to Ireland you will have great difficulty in getting a ticket to these games, but you can usually get tickets for the games leading up to the final. Gaelic matches are held throughout the country nearly every Sunday during the year. Consult the sports pages of any of the Saturday or Sunday newspapers for information on fixtures.

Rugby

Rugby Union, the amateur version of Rugby League, is played throughout the country and is particularly popular in Dublin where there are over a dozen club teams competing at senior level. The Irish international rugby team is an all-Ireland team, which competes each year for the Triple Crown (a win against England, Scotland and Wales), and the even harder Grand Slam (those same teams in addition to France). There are two home games and two away games each year, the home games being played in Lansdowne Road Stadium. These games are played in the first three months of the year and tickets are difficult to get. However, you can catch a senior club game on Saturdays in Dublin from September to April. Check the 'Sports Events' in The Irish Times on Saturday morning.

Horse Racing

Horse racing is very

popular in Ireland. In Dublin, there are bookies' shops all over the city, but of course not all of the money wagered is on Irish horses or indeed on horses racing on Irish racetracks. Every day the sports pages of the newspapers give significant coverage to the day's racing, both in Ireland and in Britain. If there is a race meeting in or near Dublin the daily newspaper is the place to look. **Leopardstown Races** are the main Dublin venue for regular meetings, but there are a number of other courses within an hour's drive from the city, notably **Fairyhouse**, where the Irish Grand National is held on Easter Monday, the **Curragh**, where the Budweiser Irish Derby is held every summer, and **Punchestown**, near Naas in County Kildare.

Soccer
Ireland is soccer mad, especially since the team reached the quarter-finals of the World Cup in Italy in 1990 and more recently its participation in the finals of the World Cup in the USA in 1994. Almost, if not all, of the players on the Irish team play for professional English clubs. In Ireland the game is still amateur and it can perhaps be seen in its truest and most basic form in the hundreds of local club games that take place every weekend between September and May. The teams competing in the Phoenix Park every Sunday during the soccer season will give you a flavour of the commitment and passion the game arouses. The top clubs play in the League of Ireland and you can get a fixture list of the matches from the **Football Association of Ireland (FAI)**, 80 Merrion Square, D2, Tel: *(01)6766864*, but the best way of finding out what matches are on is by consulting the sports pages of any of the Irish newspapers.

Annual Dublin Events

Bord Fáilte publish an annual Calendar of Events which is available at all their offices in Ireland and abroad. When in Dublin, you can consult the 'What's On' columns in the daily newspapers, *The Irish Times* being the best source for daily events in Dublin. You can also pick up a copy of the fortnightly magazine, *In Dublin*, on sale in all newsagents, or the free *Dublin Event Guide*, distributed throughout the city to selected shops, cafés, restaurants and pubs. The list of events below are regular attractions. Consult any of the above sources for exact dates.

Jan-Mar	Five Nations Rugby Championships.
Feb/Mar	Dublin Film Festival.
March	Dublin Feis Ceoil - Music Festival and Competitions from age 9 upwards. RDS Ballsbridge.
17 March	St Patrick's Day celebrations throughout the city.
Easter	Dublin Grand Opera Society Spring Season of Classic Operas. Gaiety Theatre.
Easter	Horse Racing - Annual Easter Meeting in Fairyhouse, Co. Meath.
April/May	Horse Racing - Punchestown Spring Festival Meeting, Co. Kildare.
May	Spring Show, RDS, Ballsbridge.
May	FAI Harp Lager Soccer Final. Ireland's equivalent of the famous FA Cup at Wembley, though not on such a grand scale as the Wembley event.
16 June	Bloomsday Festival - annual celebrations surrounding James Joyce's classic novel, *Ulysses*. Readings, tours, competitions, music and song - all day long.
June	GPA Music in Great Irish Houses - classical music festival in stately homes and castles, some of which are in or close to Dublin.
June	Women's Mini-Marathon - the largest women-only 10 km road race in the world.
June	Dublin International Organ and Choral Festival.
June	Budweiser Irish Derby, The Curragh, Co. Kildare.
Jun-Aug	Irish Studies Summer School, Trinity College. Tel: (01)6778117.
Jun-Aug	Residential Courses in Celtic Heritage, Trinity College. Tel: (01)2692491.
July	James Joyce Summer School, University College Dublin, Newman House.
July	Temple Bar Blues Festival.
August	Dublin Horse Show, RDS, Ballsbridge - international equestrian event.
September	All-Ireland Football and Hurling Finals in Croke Park Stadium.
October	Dublin Theatre Festival - major event in Ireland's theatre calendar.
October	Oscar Wilde Autumn School, Bray, Co. Wicklow.
October	Dublin City Marathon
October	Wicklow Mountains Walking Festival.
Nov/Dec	Dublin Grand Opera Society Winter Season of Classic Operas. Gaiety Theatre.
Christmas	Horse Racing - Four Day Festival Meeting at Leopardstown, Co. Dublin.
Monthly	Antiques & Collectables Fair, Newman House, 85 St Stephen's Green.

I N D E X